Mary Carroll

My Life

August 19, 1918

•

March 2, 2012

MARY CARROLL

This book is dedicated to the memory of the much beloved Mary Carroll of Cresco, Iowa. She will be deeply missed.

Many thanks to:

Colleen (Weber) Lang
Cheryl & Gary Weber
Kim & Creighton Weber
Joyce & Dan Regan

Editor's Notes:

This book is the text of a memoir that Mary Carroll began several years ago. She worked on it off and on for nearly a decade to tell her story and the story of the people and places around her. This is her voice. Her life in her words.

Where practical I have researched some details to provide some historical context to her experience. These are included as Endnotes. The photographs included are mostly from her memorial service in Cresco, Iowa. Other pictures are my own.

Creighton Weber's work on this project was the foundation of this project. **Thank you, Creighton**.

/Rick Regan
March 26, 2012

MARY CARROLL

EARLY DAYS

My great grandfather, James Carroll, bought a farm five miles south of Cresco, Iowa when he came from Ireland. The price was $7.50/acre and was sold by a land developer in 1858. One of his sons, John, inherited this eighty acres when his father died. My father, James Emmett was the only child of John Carroll and Elizabeth Wright. Elizabeth also came from Ireland. When she was sixteen years old she was sent to Iowa by the Lutheran Aid Society to be bound to a family to work as an indentured servant. Her father had died in New York after they arrived there and there was no money to raise a family. She never saw her family again. James Emmett was named after the famed Robert Emmett 'of Ireland. It was understood that he would live on this farm as his father left it to him when he died. There was a stipulation that he keep his mother for as long as she lived. He bought 80 acres to go with the original 80 acres for $35.00 per acre. Dad went to Catholic school in Cresco until he passed the eleventh grade. He passed the teachers exam and spent three months in Normal School in Cedar Falls so that he could teach in the country schools. It wasn't necessary that he graduate from high school.

My mother Mary (Mae) Ahern went to the same school on the other side of a board fence. We never got them to say how they got over the fence to get acquainted. The Aherns were proud Irish people who lived on the east side of Cresco. My grandfather Ahern was a railroad man, but as parents of twelve children, my grandmother "Kate" felt that they should raise the family in the country. My mother said that her mother was more of a farmer than her father was. After teaching five years in the neighboring school, Dad got married and became a farmer. They were married in 1910. They often told a story about when they got married and tried to fool their friends. They were taking the train to Minneapolis for a honeymoon. Dad hired a rig to take them to the little town of Bonair to throw off their gang of friends. The gang got on the train in Bonair[ii] before them to throw rice (or whatever they threw in those days.) As one of four children of Emmett and Mae, that is how I came to grow up on a farm south of Cresco, Iowa. My Aunt Marie told me there was great joy in the house the day I was born; the first girl after three boys. My parents never told me. In those days they were always afraid you would be spoiled, being the only girl, and the baby of the family.

My first memories are of going to school. In those days there we didn't go to kindergarten. So at six years old I could go across the field in the buggy with the rest of the family. My brother Ray drove the buggy and put the horse in the neighbor's barn until we got out of school for the day. We carried our lunch in a Karo syrup pail. We had no wax paper or Saran Wrap in those days so our sandwiches became dry before eating time. We had a slate that we wrote on with chalk. We didn't have phonics in those days, but somehow we learned to read.

The people who lived south of us were a community of Bohemian people[iii] who had come from a country called Bohemia (later referred to as Czechoslovakia and now Slovakia and the Czech Republic) and they did not speak English. All of the children in our school were Bohemian and we were the only ones who could not talk in their language. I remember my dad walking across the field one day to tell the teacher that she had to teach me separate because the other two children in my class couldn't speak English and all I did in school was chew up my books waiting for them. From then on I went ahead as I learned to read. We didn't have much fun at recess because we couldn't talk to anybody. I went there two years and then my older brother Ray was oldest to drive. We drove an old touring car to the Catholic school in Cresco[iv], the same school that my parents had gone to.

When I was six years old my mother had a birthday party for me. She asked the Baker girls that lived north of us. There were two families of Bakers. We were so bashful that day that it took us all afternoon to get acquainted. We later spent many Sunday afternoons together. When we went to high school, they rode with us. We used to walk down the road and meet and go to the Turkey River to wade and follow the trails through the woods. We never learned to swim; I guess because we never had anyone to teach us. When we were a little older, the boys in the neighborhood had a ball team. They made a ball diamond on the corner north of us in a neighbor's field. They called themselves the "Red Caps". Then the neighborhood kids would get together and watch the games. In the wintertime, we didn't see much of each other. We became better friends after we got older and could drive.

There were twenty Ahern cousins in our school at the same time. Bernice, Maureen, Marybelle and I were near the same age. We spent a lot of time staying with our cousins in town. On cold and snowy nights we stayed in town. In the summertime they came to the farm and stayed with us. When I stayed with Marybelle, in good weather we'd go roller skating on the sidewalks. They lived across from a park and we'd take our dinner to the park and pretend we had a picnic. If we could have a nickel we'd stop at the Elms Cafe and have a Coca-Cola in a 6 oz. glass which was a real treat. Bernice and Maureen lived across from a vacant lot where the circus and the tent shows set up each summer. These were traveling shows. I never got to go to one because I either didn't have the money or else I wasn't there at the right time. Instead we played "show" and chorus girls for hours. At Aunt Blanche's house we had a chorus line in the kitchen with Aunt Blanche playing the piano. How we did learn to do the kick! Silent movies were in then. I only saw one. It was "Freckles". Later shows became a very important part of our entertainment.

MARY CARROLL

After church on Sundays we cousins all gathered at the Ahern garage. We had three uncles who sold Overland and Whippet Cars'. We stayed around there for about an hour. Sometimes Aunt Marie was cooking up a picnic. She liked to get us all to go to Vernon Springs and take our meal. We'd take our swimming suits, but we were never allowed to go into the deep water. The garage always had boxes of candy bars on the counter, but none of us ever had a nickel to buy any. We never asked for money because we knew there was no extra money - This of course was during the Depression. I think I craved those Milky Ways all my life - I never got over wanting them.

When I was in the third grade, we went to school in town. We had very strict nuns for teachers. I was real good in Math, but I hated History. We rode in a touring car with Ray driving. A touring car was called that because it was open and had no windows.

Sometimes in the winter, if we couldn't get through the roads we used a horse drawn sled. It took about an hour to get there. Ray and Gene had to take the horses to a barn near the school and tie them up until we went home. We stayed in town with Grandma Carroll or the cousins. We thought it was awfully quiet at Grandma's house. We had our own Carroll Grandma, the Ahern one we had to share. We could get library books when we stayed in town. We couldn't have our own library card because our township didn't pay for it. We had to sneak them. Sometimes Grandma had us come to dinner at her house and we didn't have to eat out of the dinnerpail. (Dinner was at noon) It always tasted better at her house. She'd fix it up nice for us with cloth napkins and tablecloths and we thought that was style. We didn't get many presents in those days, but Grandma Carroll gave us each a $1.00 for our birthday.

Being a farm kid was not the highlight of my life....

Town kids never had to worry that the hay would all be up by the fourth of July so they could go to the celebration. They didn't have to carry their lunch in a pail or go home to do chores.

8

People would say "but your dad owns a farm." That didn't mean anything to me. When farm girls were learning the art of gardening, I was learning the piano. My mother wanted to play the piano so badly. When I took lessons, she would take my books and try to do the same things. She taught herself to play by notes instead of by ear as she previously had.

She was disappointed that I didn't become good at it. She said I took after my Dad and didn't have music in my soul. I didn't mind because Dad and I got along just fine. Aunt Marie taught us how the "city ladies wore feathers in their hats" and how to have lace on your shawl. We got lots of fancy ideas from knowing her. She came from Chicago and we thought that gave her an edge. I knew that you always wore hats, gloves and shoes to match. I didn't know that our parsnips were not dug until spring, but I knew that you didn't wear a white hat until after the 15th of August. My mother was frail and wanted me to help her in the house. One day she decided I should learn how to milk a cow if I needed to. She sent me to the barn without doing the supper dishes one evening. I sat on the swing on the old oak tree (my thinking place until the milking was done...by that time the dishes were too. Nobody noticed that I never learned how to milk a cow.

We didn't have pretty clothes. Mom's sister lived in Chicago and sent her old ones to me. We made them over and somehow made do. I had a 2nd cousin who was a nurse (on the Carroll side) who sent me hand me downs. They were not appropriate for a child, but we had no money for clothes. My mother instilled in me that I should work before I got married so I could have nice clothes and things for myself. She always said "Clothes make the man" and she believed that you had to be well dressed to get ahead. She didn't have many pretty things for herself at the time. I am glad she lived to see the time when Dad could buy nice things for the house and pretty dresses for her. We always had nice Christmases. We didn't have much for presents, but we always made a holiday out of it. Going to church was the most important part. Mother took boughs from the grove and formed a background for a crib. She would decorate this and we had a Christmas corner.

After the chores were done on Christmas Eve we would gather there and sing carols whiles she played the piano. We each had a present like warm gloves, or a stocking cap or a sweater etc. We would hang our stocking on the open staircase when we were young enough to believe in Santa. We had to stop at Grandma Carroll's after church because Santa came there too. I used to get a doll or toy dishes or something to wear. Then she would come to our house for Christmas dinner which was always special. When we went to Grandma Ahern's we used to play the piano. There were old World War I songs on sheet music in her piano bench. Aunt Blanche was a good player and she taught her girls to play. Marybelle and I took lessons from the nuns. We all sang together with Aunt Blanche playing.

One time we saw her line a pan with biscuit dough, fill it with creamed chicken and cover it with more dough. There was enough for all the cousins and uncles and aunts. The Ahern uncles were real good ball players. We always had a good game of baseball when we got there in the field. I remember when Uncle John came from Florida for Grandpa and Grandma Ahern's 50th wedding anniversary. I was 7 years old and made my first communion that day. They had a Roosevelt Marman car[vi] and the girl's had socks that matched their dresses. That was real "rich". Grandpa died soon after that. He was a lot older than grandma.

I don't think the word "depression" was used in the 1930's. It was only called "the depression" when it was talked about later. I didn't know that times could be any different. I had never seen the time when people had money to buy things with. Our going to school in Cresco put a great strain on our folk's income.

They wanted us to have a Catholic education. They had a car on the road for many years. It was important to them that we go to high school. Many of our neighbors' kids didn't get to go. There were no school buses. Some family's paid for a ride with us. One family paid for the girl and the son caught rides wherever he could. One family often sent the kids out when they saw us coming down the road. Nothing was ever said. We knew they didn't have the money to pay. We piled them in and they became good friends.

Years later this family had a job to give and I got it. I felt fully repaid.

When we went to school in our old Overland car, we put 2 cream cans in between the seats and took the cream to the creamery in town before we went to school. A couple of times a week we took a 2 lb crock with us and the buttermaker ladled butter into it. Not all the farmers bought butter. Some made their own with the cream before they sold it. Dad thought that the creamery made better butter than we did.

Butter was very important as a staple on the table. We had neighbors across the road who had several daughters who were marriageable age. On Sunday nights one of the girls would come over and borrow butter. They had boyfriends for supper and wanted to make a good impression. On Monday they brought the butter back. Mom didn't like it very well, but I think she felt pride in helping them all get husbands. There were no cooking oils, no vegetable shortenings. We used cream for cakes and cookies and lard for frying and pies. The eggs were my mother's source of grocery money. We didn't buy much at the store. We had our vegetables, fruit and meat on the farm. We bought flour, sugar, cocoa, coffee, oatmeal and etc. Some people said they ate lots of oatmeal and cornmeal mush during the hard years.

We had more pancakes, eggs, chickens and homemade bread than cereals. Mom made very good yeast bread, baking powdered biscuits and pancakes from scratch. We planted lots of potatoes. I always thought potatoes could only be dug on Saturdays. They saved that job for children on Saturdays. It was a big job. The horses pulled a wagon in the field and we filled it up. They were put into a big pile in the cellar. We had vegetables from our garden. Mom wanted fruit trees so we'd have something for pies. They planted lots of apple trees, plum trees and grapevines. We used wild choke cherries, elderberries and such for jelly. We ate real well but it was more work to get it.

In the winter the men butchered a beef. It was cut into chunks on the kitchen table and put on the ice in the milk house. It would freeze and we would cook a big chunk if there were a lot of people or slice some and fry it if there were only a few. There were no roasts and steaks and such. Sometimes it was browned and canned to be used in the summer when we couldn't keep it cold.

It was only in the late 30's that we had regular cuts of meat when the lockers were invented and the farmer took their meat there to be processed. Then it was labeled. Steaks and French fries were not known to Iowa kids until they went to war and they got to restaurants away from home. When they butchered a pig the meat was fried down into patties and sealed with lard covering it. That way it kept in the cellar because it was sealed. The first pork chop I ever ate was at a friend's house. Her mother worked at the A & P and they had meat from the butcher shop there. I didn't tell them, though' I had never tasted anything so good. I was in high school.

We made a chocolate cake with cream for shortening and a white cake with butter. I think we acquired a taste for chocolate because cocoa was cheaper that other flavorings.

Our income came from the pigs that were sold and the cream that was taken to the creamery to be made into butter. The crops were fed to the livestock. Mom had $2 or $3 egg money per week (money obtained from selling eggs) to buy groceries for the six of us.

The original farm contract that said Dad should pay Grandma Carroll $500 per year for the farm had to be broken. He borrowed money to fix her house into another apartment. She rented out two rooms and a bath for $15/month. This was her living. Dad paid the bigger bills like insurance and coal and taxes. It was many years before he was able to pay off that loan. When Dad sold hogs, he stopped at a butcher shop and bought "beef steaks" and the grocer usually threw in chocolate drops.

For many years Dad had a $4000 debt on the farm. Many a time I saw him sit at the kitchen table with his head in his hands and a tear in his eye when he couldn't see how he could make his bills. Evidently he needed more money one day. Mother was to go to the bank and sign some papers. She and I walked around and around the block past the bank. She was crying and she said "I won't sign it. They will have our farm if we put a mortgage on it." Dad was in the bank waiting for her. Finally she had to give in and go in. In 1937 Dad was 51 years old and he quit farming. He tried several things. He ran for County auditor and didn't make it. He was a bookkeeper for a garage and a bill collector. The people he contacted told him that the garage owner owed them more bills that they did. He tried demonstrating gasoline powered washing machines to farmers' wives. He never did a wash in his life....I guess he didn't sell too many.

Farmers saved their best corn for seed to plant the next year. Just at that time hybrid seed corn was brought into the scene. Dad got the job of selling and he really found his niche. He sold Funk's G Hybrid seed corn[vii] until he was 80 years old. He did real well. When Roosevelt came into power the Federal Land Bank[viii] was started. Dad got a 33 year loan on the farm and he became a different person. He gave Henry Wallace[ix] and FDR[x] the credit for saving his farm & bringing prosperity to the Iowa Farmer. They stayed on the farm until 1945 when Ray came home from the war to take over operating the farm.

In 1945 the farm house was wired for electricity[xi]. After the war it was turned on. It was shocking to see the back of the closets! That was also a New Deal project.

We had a cistern for our water. The water ran off the roof when it rained into eave troughs that lead into the cistern. There was a small pump in the house. If you didn't use too much and it rained a lot in the summer, we had water enough for all winter.

The drinking water was carried from the well. You didn't drink cistern water. Sometimes we strained it to wash our hair. It might have leaves and things from the roof.

On the coal and wood range in the kitchen was a reservoir. You filled this every morning and you had hot water for dishes and etc. When we washed, we pumped enough to fill a boiler and put it on the range to heat. You then cut up a bar of laundry soap into shavings and heated it with hot water until it was melted. Then you pailed the water and soap into the washer. The washer was on the back porch and had a belt that went to a gas engine on the ground. It wasn't an easy day. People didn't change their clothes as often as they do now. Ironing was harder because we had to heat flat irons on the range.

My mother got a good price for her eggs during the war. We still lived on the farm after Dad quit farming and we had our living there. Mom was able to put enough of her egg money away so that one day she and I went to town. She wanted a house in town. With $2800 she bought a two bedroom home with a furnace, hot and cold running water and electricity. She rented it a few years to others and when the war was over, they moved in. They then had the money to buy a lot of things they went without all those years.

I guess we had a pretty good time as teenagers. We knew a lot of kids from quite a ways around. I was fortunate that I had Jerry and Gene to do the driving. Girls didn't drive by themselves then. They were always good to take me along. Even when they had a date they had me tagging along. About 20 of us used to go to house parties. We would dance or play cards at each other's houses. Some belonged to the Lutheran League, some to the Methodist young people's group and some were Catholics. We learned to dance at these places to a mouth organ, a piano or sometimes and accordion. We learned to do the circle two-step, the square dance and the fox trot. When midnight came the parents passed around numbers and you drew for partners for supper. That was the way they got they boys from one side of the room and the girls from the other. When I was 16 I was allowed to go to Vernon Springs to dances. Prohibition[xii] was repealed that year but the 3.2 beer [xiii]didn't reach around there then. We were too young so it didn't become an issue with us. Eventually they roped off part of the pavilion and put tables where they served beer. Hard liquor wasn't served in public in Iowa for years.

People bought 7-Up and carried their own bottles of whiskey and mixed it under the table. It wasn't a problem with our group. I guess we didn't have the money to buy it. This was the time the cousins stayed with us, because they didn't have a driver.

Bernice was our hairdresser when we got ready to go to a dance. If anyone had a nickel they would go to the mill in town and get flax seed. We'd boil it in some water, strain it and it was a stiffening to set our hair with. That's how our hair was waved.

One day we were dismissed from school soon after we got there. Our folks thought we were in school. Marybelle's brother Ray had been with a scout group who found a cave[xiv] up near Harmony, MN. He wanted to show it to the rest of us. Ten of us got in two cars and we went to explore. It had not been discovered long, but there were slimy ropes and ladders in there. There were 3 levels and some waterfalls over 100' deep. We took two lanterns and 3 flashlights.

We didn't have science enough in high school to know that when the lanterns went out that we didn't have air enough to breathe. We spent an hour in there pushing each other up the ropes and jumping over ledges that had some awful drops on the other side. Later this cave was opened to the public and we were shocked to see where we had been.

One of the highlight in my high school days was the time I was voted May Queen. Each year one of the senior girls was picked to crown the Blessed Virgin statue at church. It was on a high pedestal in church. I wore a borrowed wedding gown with a train. Three marriages and it was the only time I ever wore a wedding gown!

Part of the New Deal from FDR was the CCC camp[xv]. Young men who had no work were put in camps and lived in barracks and given park work to do. Cresco had one of these camps. They were young people like the one in our neighborhood, but we were forbidden to know them. On Saturday night, a group of CCC's stood on one corner in town and girls on another. Some girls we knew went with them, but we were not allowed. There were more parks and trails in Decorah than at Cresco. They were moved to Decorah and they did wonderful things there to build dams and waterways. It was all hand work. When we went on picnics from school or when the Aherns got together, we usually went to the parks in Decorah. They built trails and walks through the woods.

One winter we rented 2 rooms in town near the school. The roads were not open all the time them.

We got to go to some basketball games that we didn't see when we went home every night. My mother had an uncle in Red Wing, MN. His kids were our age. His son was alone at a boarding house during the summer.

He asked Mom to take him to the farm. His mother was dead. Pat came down for some time every summer when he was a teen. One time some of his friends from Red Wing came to see him. They asked me to spend some time with them in Red Wing. I went with Lucille for a week. They were on their own and we really saw Red Wing. They had bars before Iowa, so they had to show me the brass rail where the factory workers went on Saturday nights. I met one of their friends and he asked me to go to the show. I guess that was my first date. He was tall and handsome and I was pretty flattered.

When I went back to school I really let the girls know I had met someone wonderful. Several months later we got a call that he had arrived in Cresco on the midnight train. O boy! What I didn't tell. He and Jerry and I were riding around downtown at noon. We stopped in front of the theater. All of a sudden Francis was out of the car and running down Main Street. A man was running after him screaming "Francis! Francis!" It turned out that he had run away from home. I went back to school embarrassed to death. For several months I got letters from his mother with clippings from a magazine with stories about bad girls who caused good boys to stray from their calling to the priesthood. Several years later he came back again. He found work among the farmers in the summertime. One day then Dad got a call about him from the local clothing store owner. He had given him a bad check and left town. I never heard from him again.

When I was in high school I chose to take a business course. I disliked History and Geography. I took two years of bookkeeping, typing and shorthand. I wanted to be a bookkeeper.

Had I planned to be a teacher, I should have take a Normal course for two years at the public school. I had no such plans. I was going to the city and be in an office. There were no jobs when I got out and it was hard to start out on your own without any money. First I got a job with my dad measuring fields for the government farm program. We measured farmers' fields, one by one with a steel tape. We had a board in the back seat of the car where we drew the fields to scale. I made $45 that fall. I bought a brown tweed coat and a brown felt hat. That was all I made.

I got a job at the local hospital carrying trays, doing what nurses' aides do now. I was to get $15 a month and my board and room. Dad didn't think much of that so he went to the school board meeting across the field and became the director. As director he could hire the teacher! They paid $60/month the first year and $65/mo. the second year. I had to go three months to Normal school[xvi] in Cedar Falls. I borrowed $125 from the bank and spent the summer there. Grace, a classmate of mine went too. We were roommates at a rooming house. We ate on $.50 a day. We had coffee and roll --$.10-- plate lunch--$.25-- hot dog and milk--$.15. I just barely passed the history course as I knew no history at all. We took Management and Methods. In Management, we learned how to start a fire. Methods didn't tell us much about a country school, especially not how to teach 8 grades! It really wasn't much preparation. We had to pass the state exams, too. I did proceed to teach for six years. I had schools where the children didn't speak English when they started school. When I was in my 4th year my superintendent came to visit my school. He called me outside after he had sat in on my classes and said, "Mary, you are now a school teacher!" There were years that I really enjoyed it and became quite learned in History as well. I even had a rhythm band. My early music came in very useful as

17

we used it so often. We had many songs and music games when the day was so dark that we couldn't see to read. We had no electricity, lights, water or inside toilets.

My brother was always bringing home guys who were looking for work. Bob was one of them. Dad and some neighbors hired him when they need help. I guess I decided everyone should have a boyfriend and Bob was handy. He was from Illinois. I went with him for a while. I took his ring and thought we'd get married.

 About that time 3 teachers were going to California and looking for a 4th to share expenses. They asked me to join them. I did and we had a time of our lives. We went 7000 miles in 6 weeks. We each took $100. We went to Washington state and then down the coast to Mexico and home through Colorado and Nebraska. We went to a lot of relatives and made many new friends. When I got home, I had a letter from Bob...He was in southern Illinois working in a coal mine. I decided if I could go to California I didn't need to marry a coal miner.

My school was closed when that fall started because of a lack of students. My dad was president of the Federal Land Bank. They needed a girl in the office. The vice-president had a daughter too. We shared the job. We went every other day. We made $2.00/day. I was happy in that job, but it wasn't very profitable. The superintendent called and wanted me to go to Elma to teach. I went in November. That was the year of the *1940 blizzard*[vii]. I boarded in the country and walked 2 miles to the school. It was the most lonesome place I had ever been. I didn't know anyone. I had broken up with my boyfriend in Mankato, Mn. Eventually, I got a job in a cafe working for my board and I had a room with a nice couple near the school. I was in my glory. I loved it and I loved the work I was doing.

I was ready for a new job in a year. I went to school in Mankato and there were 500 students in the same room doing bookkeeping. We had bulbs hanging from the ceiling. The lighting was very poor. I didn't have real good eyes. One day after 6 months I was blind in one eye. I went to the eye doctor. He told me I needed to have my glassed changed because of strain. I didn't believe him. I went home to my regular doctor. He sent me to Rochester.

He told me to get there as fast as I could. He thought I was going blind, he said. They couldn't find anything wrong except the strain. They changed my glasses every three months for a year and told me not to ever do bookkeeping again. I wished I had changed my glasses in Mankato and never gone home.

I eventually went on to teach 2 more years. I think I became a good school teacher. We had some very good times when I went back to the Elma school. I didn't have to teach them English first. My eight grade pupils all passed the state exams wherever I taught.

Later I did become a bookkeeper. I was the bookkeeper for Bergfalk[xviii] furniture store for 5 years. I kept the entire set of books and was very proud that when the auditor came every year, he didn't change a thing.

That was where I met Gerald Regan who was a country school teacher. That and the rest of my life is another chapter. War came next.

MARY CARROLL

GERALD REGAN

I thought I cut quite a figure walking down that ice crusted road just after dawn. My green plaid snow suit with the peaked cap was new. I don't think a soul ever saw me. I never saw a car on that road in the morning. It was with a tear in my eye and regret that I had signed that contract to teach in the country school northeast of Elma. There were houses on side roads, but I had no idea who lived in them. I guess it was a chore time so nobody else was out.

There was a director from the local community elected to run each school. If you had a good Director he mowed the grass once in the fall, filled the woodshed with corn cobs and coal to burn during the winter. If you were lucky, you got a ball and bat. I had a very good director. His wife washed the sash curtains before I got there. It was their job too to board the teacher if there was no other place for the teacher to stay. They had a nice home and they were good people. The only room left for me had no heat, but they had electricity and hot and cold running water. These things I didn't have at home.

When I got to school, the coal stove had to be started with the cobs and paper in the waste basket from the day before. The mice ran under your feet before you got them into the stove. The corncobs and bread crusts in the waste basket made a feast after we left.

Mrs. Lauck provided me with a good breakfast before I left and packed a nice lunch. She had a good supper ready when I got home about 5 o'clock in the evening. They processed their own meat and sent it to Protivin for summer sausage to be made by a farmer who did that in the winters. (Polashek[xix]) I had never eaten it before. With her good home-made bread and goodies that she baked, I had a tasty lunch. I never bothered that much when I came from home. For this I paid $1.00 per day.

In time the children became people and we got very interested in what we were doing. I had 22 children, many of them I the upper grades. We were very seriously worked to be able to pass the Iowa state tests that they were going to pass before they could go to high school. For many of them this was the end of their school days. We didn't have much equipment. We made games out of maps and music lessons. On the dark days we tried to do things from memory as we had no lights. At recess in the winter, we had checker tournaments and music from our Victrola[xx]. I never thought to ask for new records. I guess there was no one to ask. I found a *rhythm band*[xxi] somewhere and we had a lot of fun with that. We played "Pop goes the Weasel" until we nearly wore it out.

At this time my social life was nil. I had broken up with the man I was going to marry. I had friends that I went places with, but not anybody special. I had a friend who made a date with me the first week I was there and stood me up. I sure took a beating from my class on that one. They almost crowded the door to see him. He had a good excuse and came the next week. I was so anxious for a cigarette when he got there, I asked him to stop at the general store so that I could get a package. (10 cents) I got a good talking to about ladies smoking. Little did we know then what harm they could do.

For school I wore cotton blouses with wool skirts. I had a blue, yellow and a pink blouse. I bought them for 50 cents each at the Penney store in Cresco. I made $82.50 a month that year. I got 50 cents extra because I had a class of over 15 pupils. The girls who worked in the stores and offices in town got $10/week. We had grades 1 through 8 plus primary. (Primary was our version of kindergarten.) We didn't have much training to do this. I guess we followed the pattern of what we did when we went to school. I enjoyed it when we got into it.

The Laucks had a hired man to help with the farming. He was a young fellow about my age. He smoked a cigarette after each meal and one before he went to bed. One night I asked him to wait until the family went to bed so I could have one of his cigarettes. It was a hard pull. "He didn't spend any of his money on a girl unless he intended to marry her." After that I carried 5 cigarettes in a cough drop box in my briefcase. Every night I went out to the outhouse after school and had a cigarette. I don't know why I didn't just quit.

When my dad came for me on Friday night, I smoked until I went back Monday morning. Many times Mrs. Lauck said to me "I don't think teachers should smoke, do you?" I always agreed with her.

There were young people in the neighborhood that Mrs. Lauck thought the hired man and I should get to know. She wanted me to have a hard working farmer and she picked one out for me. One family that had 3 sons got invited to a card party. I don't know whether they knew what was up, the sons never showed up. She insisted that the hired man call a young lady down the road. They started a romance and he eventually married her. He used to say he was going to save his money for his old age.

I didn't know I had an old age coming, so it never entered my mind. He did own a small farm when he got old and they go south every winter so maybe he had a point. I think it was the wife's inheritance that helped him buy the farm. I had plans for an Irishman who didn't have a farm. I wasn't a farmer and I wasn't looking for one.....

As time went on we were required to have meetings in our district in our school houses. We had county meetings every month for the teachers in the county. These were held in different towns.

There were 99 teachers in the county. These were held in different towns. There were 99 teachers in the county. 96 of them were women. When we had a meeting at my school, I was pleased that an Irishman was teaching in the school next to mine. We got acquainted at these meetings and visited a lot. I heard he had a girl in Riceville who had long black hair and was very pretty. I saw them at the show one Sunday night in Cresco and found this to be true.

In those days the bands that became the big names started in the bigger halls in the Midwest. We danced to Ted Weems, Lawrence Welk, Glen Miller, Cab Calloway and Jimmy Dorsey. There were cowboy bands in the little towns and at wedding dances. *Spillville* [xvii] was the place to go if you wanted a big band for a special date. My friend Gerald Regan was a fan of the *Hit Parade* [xviii] and loved to dance. He was 6'2" and very good looking and a very good dancer. We talked about the music that made the *Hit Parade* each week and where the bands were going to be.

On Sunday nights one went to the theater and the weeknights were for dancing. If you went to the show, you were to go to the ice cream parlor after for a sundae. The most popular was chocolate with marshmallow topping. That is, if you didn't have a fellow who wanted to save his money for his old age. After the dance you went to the nearest joint for burgers and coffee or beer. Fellow didn't take girls to dinner in our circles. You were free to dance with all of your friends, but the last dance before intermission and the last dance of the evening belonged to your date. We usually knew everybody in the hall and you exchanged dances with a lot of people.

It was special night when Gerald Regan called and asked me to go to the next dance in Spillville. I walked on air for a while. This was the Irishman I was looking for. He had broken up with the girl in Riceville. I gave my brothers orders that "this is one that you don't say the wrong thing to." Just stay out of my way and don't spoil it for me. They were pretty good at saying the wrong things and this time was mine. The bells never stopped ringing from then on.

Gerald Regan was a serious teacher. After he finished high school he went to Riceville for a year of Normal Training. With that he could teach in the country schools. I didn't get Normal Training in high school. I went to Teachers College one quarter to get my certificate. When they told us that we would receive surplus government food to give our students he objected loudly. "Nobody in his school needed the government to feed them" he said. We were given grapefruit juice, peanut butter, kidney beans and butter. They brought bread and we made peanut butter sandwiches. The butter didn't keep very well and we had no refrigerator. Gerald finally had to give in and serve the food.

He was interested in literature and poetry. He also liked math and history. While in Riceville, he boarded at the funeral home. He worked for his board by driving the ambulance and helping with funerals. In order to be licensed funeral director, he had to apprentice with a funeral home and spend a year in St. Louis at school and then spend another year apprenticing again. These were his plans when I married him.

In the summer of 1941, my brothers Gene and Ray were in school in Madison, Wisc. Ray was older as he worked for a while to get money for school. The *draft* xxiv was put in place as war was getting closer. Gene was one of the first to have to go. The war was to change all of the plans of the young men at the time. Ray was called even though he was in his 30's. War seemed far away from us. We didn't think it could hurt us. We were too busy planning the rest of our lives. Gerald and I spent as much time as we could together that year. He had a *Model A Ford* xxv. If we went close he drove his Ford. If a dance was in order, his father reluctantly lent us the family car. This had to be spaced out so as not to be too extravagant. It was on a Sunday night when he came to take me to the show which our world turned upside down. We were told during the day to listen to the President Roosevelt at 7 pm on the radio. He told of Pearl Harbor being bombed and war being declared. Gerald was 21 years old and he had no reason to be deferred. We both cried that night and knew it was to affect us badly.

WAR

It wasn't long before things started to change. Draft boards were formed in every county. A representative of each area was on the board. Ration books were made out. The children had new words to learn-- sabotage--traitor--and the like. We made out the ration books for our district *in our schools* [xxvi].

Tires, sugar, gas and meat were rationed. They were not any of my worries. We didn't drive a lot or care if we didn't have sugar. Farmers were allowed to use the meat they raised. We had bigger worries. If you were a farmer you were need to plant more food for soldiers and were deferred[xxvii]. Gerald didn't have much plan to farm. His dad had bought a farm late in life and hoped he would help him on it. He helped put in the crop in spring and take it out in the fall. This was for his dad's sake. It was not his plan to farm. Some young people became farmers very quickly. If they had a city job, dad brought them back to the help with the farm. Those people were resented when they didn't have to go to the war. Nobody objected to farm boys who intended to farm getting deferments. Cigarettes were hard to get, but if you had a few friends in the stores you usually could get a couple of packs a week. They wanted to be sure that the soldier boys had a lot of them. Never did we know what damage they would do. We knew Gerald had no reason to be deferred. Gerald didn't sign a contract to teach that spring. We knew we couldn't make many plans, but we knew we would be together. On the 4th of July went on a picnic to Decorah. Decorah was always the place to picnic. They had lovely parks and wooded trails. Along one of these trails, Gerald gave me a diamond ring. All of our dreams had come true. We were going to be married as soon as we found out what was in store for us.

That fall Gerald asked the man on the draft board when he would be called. He told him we planned to be married and we would like to know where he stood. He said "you can go on the next draft." When Gerald got back from his physical and was signed into the army, he met the same man again and was told "You wouldn't have had to go you know!" Gerald said he never came as close to flooring a man before. [xxviii]

Those were sad days in November. It wasn't long until the order came to be on the bus in Cresco on a certain evening. It was the last week of Thanksgiving that we saw them off on a bus. It was a hard time. Nothing good was ahead of them. The first I heard was that he was in an army camp in Fort Worth, Texas and would be for 3 months of basic training.

All of the boys that we knew were getting called. Some of the girls who were free went to work where there was war work to do. The north was being vacated and everybody was moving south. The service camps were in the warmer climate and in areas that were not usable for farming to feed the men. My brother Jerry had had a heart attack in his young years and was granted a *deferment*[xxix]. It was called 4F if you were not physically able to serve. First the boys were given a basic training that was pretty rugged. Then they were assigned to a unit or to more extensive training. You didn't get any choice of where you wanted to be. Gerald was given 3 choices of what type of unit he wanted. He asked for a medical assignment. His papers came back --Infantry--Infantry--Infantry.

MARY CARROLL

It was quite a surprise when Gerald wrote that he had an aunt in Fort Worth and I could come and spend Christmas with him there. There were other teachers who were going too and spend the week at the guest house. My Christmas program would be ending on the night we were to take the train at midnight from Elma to Texas. It would cost $25, take 24 hours and we would be there just before Christmas.

It was a thrill just to think of such a thing. One girl I knew couldn't come with us because they were going to save their money to start farming. Again, I was glad I wasn't planning to start farming.

For the Christmas Program, Mr. Lauck went early to the school house to light the oil lamp that hung from the ceiling and stoke up the fire. The hired man took the rest of us with the team and sled. It was a bitter cold night. A sheet closed off our stage. Each child had a piece in the program and we had some skits. After an exchange of gifts (the children had previously drawn names) it was finally over.

I could hardly wait. The trains were so crowded and late at that time because of the soldiers who rode them. We were 12 hours late getting into Fort Worth. The soldier boys stayed up all night except one who went to sleep. When the train pulled in, that fellow was fresh and the only one who met our train. Gerald felt quite proutd when he got all the honor of being there when we pulled in.

We took the bus to his Aunt Winnie's. When the bus was empty at the end of the line, the driver said, "Soldier, just where was it that you wanted to go!" Gerald said, "We'll just go around again until we see the place." The bus driver knew we were from the country. It was unbelievable to me that it was so warm. There were rose garden all around the city. It was quite a change from where we had come from. We had a wonderful Christmas. I brought him a camera to take pictures of the places where he would be. It had the first flash that we had ever seen. He had a ladies billfold that was a real treasure to me. It was blue and had a red lining. Perfumes were some of the things he brought back for me. After Christmas he had to go back to camp. I took the bus to the camp and then to the guest house. It was dark when the bus arrived. I thought of the folks back home who had fretted because we had to spend the holidays at an army camp. The Christmas lights in Fort Worth were the most spectacular sight I had ever seen.

The lights of Fort Worth and army camp astounded me. After the one oil lamp I had in my school for the program I couldn't believe what I was seeing. Under different circumstances the army camp would have been a good experience for them. With war so close, it made it hard to enjoy. The guest house was like the barracks. There were 2 cots to a room. Whoever came in was your roommate. I roomed with a soldier's wife from Kentucky. She was real interesting. I think we stayed for a $1.00 per night. No soldiers were allowed. After New Years Eve with the boys we had to go back home. I hated to leave that midnight. We never knew when we would see them again. One of the teachers went home, packed up her things, quit teaching and went back in a couple of weeks. Her soldier was quarantined for 3 weeks with the measles. She had to spend the time in a room off camp. They were married the next week-end in the camp chapel.

Gerald spent 3 months in basic training. Instead of doing *KP*[xxx] like all soldiers did, he was teaching *illiterates*[xxxi] to read and write. He was given a chance to go to officers training. He signed up for this and it took him to Fort Benning, Ga. Ordinarily to be a 2nd Lieutenant, you went to West Point for 4 years. A very difficult training, both physical and mental was given at this time. Only a small percentage of the boys passed. The wives couldn't go. They were out in the field most of the time, hiking, camping in swamps etc. My brother Ray took the same training in Virginia at the same time. He was small physically and older. He didn't make it. There were pretty hard feelings over this.

He was sent to an outpost in *Panama*[xxxii] and stayed there the rest of the war. They had wanted to get married and he never got home until 1945 when our grandmother died and he got to come

29

home for that. They were married on the week-end that he got home.

In July of 1943, Gerald was to be through with officers training. We would not know if he made it until the last minute. If he made it, I was allowed to be there to pin the 2 gold bars on the shoulders of my lieutenant. If he made it, he would get a furlough and we could get married. If he didn't, he wouldn't get home. We had to be called in both churches each Sunday for 3 weeks, get a blood test and the marriage license. That also meant get a wedding dress, dinner and other plans. There were so many ifs, it was hard to make plans.

Weddings were not big in my family. Marriages were. You got one choice and it was for life. You best pick the one you wanted. Gerald wrote "You go to the priests and get the license and if I make it, we'll be married when I get home. Don't pay any attention to what my folks say. I have always done what they told me, but from here on I do what I want. Don't let them talk you out of it." I stopped at the Regan's on my way to see the Elma priest. They did everything they could to get me to wait until Gerald got home and see what he had to say about it. Then they thought one of them should go with me. I eased out of there as best I could, saying that I didn't need anyone. The priest in Cresco put me at ease. He said "You are going to marry him, it doesn't matter if you are called ahead in case you can't now."

I had everything ready. My dad said he'd buy me a wedding dress. I never planned on a wedding gown. I couldn't find what I wanted in Cresco, so one day Mom and Dad and I went to Waterloo. I got a gold silk dress with big pearl buttons. It cost $20. It would go with his army uniform. If he was a 2nd lieutenant, he would get a much nicer uniform. The pants were called "pinks" and the coat was not the khaki of soldiers. They were brown with a pinkish cast. The ladies had a shower for me on the day I expected to hear from him. I didn't hear a word they said until the telephone rang and the operator read the telegram that he sent. We didn't have good long distance calling back then. It said "I made it, I'm on my way." I nearly cried in front of all of them. Needless to say,

I didn't get to Georgia to pin the bars on his shoulders. An officer could live off camp with his wife. He got more pay and had more time off. We saved $100/month. That was more than we normally got for wages. There were not too many to come to my wedding. A lot of the people we knew were about the war business. Helen Crowe was my bridesmaid. Barney Beecher was his best man.

We were married on a Saturday morning a 8 o'clock. There were about 25 people to come to the farm for dinner. My mother and I set the dining room table with the best silver, linens and goblets that we had. We had 2 card tables set in the living room. My aunt Aletha and Jerry sang. I was so excited; I never heard a note of the songs. My grand-mothers, Jerry's family, Gerald's sister and family and the 2 priests made up our guests.

Of course my parents and his were also present. A lady came and brought the chicken dinner and also made a wedding cake.

We had a soldier and his bride on the cake top. We decorated the tables with flags. Later in the afternoon Gerald and I took his dad's car and took off. We never told anyone where we went because we only had until Monday morning that we could stay.

My folks took us to Jerry's house. There was a lieutenant from Monona, IA that was in Gerald's unit and they were both due in Camp Wolters at Tyler, Texas. Lt Leibenstein took his car to Texas and asked us to ride. We had a nice trip to Texas. It took us 3 days.

Gerald had a friend name Ed Lentz. He was in the army before Gerald. He wrote to us and asked us to write to him. My friend Anna Grace was not going with anyone at the time. She said, "Let me write to him." When Ed came home we arranged for her to meet him. We got a letter on our wedding day that they were married the same day that we were in Harrisburg, Pa. They were married two weeks prior to when he was shipped overseas. It was 2 years before she saw him again. He was in some terrific fighting and went through allot. While we were still in Texas, Lt.

Leibenstein was shipped overseas. He wasn't there very long when he was killed in the terrible fight in Italy.

Gerald gave me a string of pearls that I wore for our wedding. I gave him a gold and black cigarette case. He carried those cigarettes and I hope it keep them dry. On our wedding day Gerald said to me "You are my wife and you shall have anything you want."

I found a room in Tyler, Texas. I talked to a girl that I met along the way. She knew of a Mrs. Long who rented most of her house to soldiers. She spent the summer on her screened-in back porch. She gave another couple and us the use of the kitchen and a bedroom each. For this we paid $28.00 a month. It was 120 degrees that summer. It was terribly hot for us, but the boys went on 20 mile long hikes and trained outdoors. It was a terrible long walk for Gerald to get the bus to go to camp. There were lines a block long waiting. We had a good time in Tyler, Texas. We spent 2 months there. It was different for me and our new life together. One day he got orders to report to *Camp Polk, La.* [xxxiii] Gerald came in that night very upset. He was sure this was his time to go to combat. Wives were not allowed to go to Camp Polk. He cried all that night. He said he was not trained or ready to go. We had to go by bus to Dallas and I was to go home from there. Looking for a room in a hotel that night he ran into guys with *woodchopper badges* [xxxiv] on their sleeves. That was the outfit he was to join in Louisiana. He asked them were they were headed and they told him that the woodchoppers were going to Camp to go on maneuvers. We found a room for the night and then went out and ate the biggest steak we could find. That wasn't bad news at all. I took the train and went home to Cresco for two months.

Gerald came and got me at Thanksgiving. Then we went to *Camp Clayborne in Alexandria, La.* [xxxv] There was a car sitting at a gas station in Elma with a for sale sign on it. Gerald and I went in and bought it. It was so far to camp from our rooms that he took all his time to get home. His folks and sister gave him the greatest talking to. He didn't need a car when he had buses to ride. He was 23 years old. Then we drove back to camp. It was a gold *Studebaker* [xxxvi]. It was probably 2 or 3 years old. H paid $500 for it.

When we got to La. the rooming houses were so full you couldn't find a room anywhere. We started walking down the streets carrying a suitcase. At on house, a soldier and his wife were moving out. He hollered, "Soldier, are you looking for a room?" That was where I stayed for the 5 months that I was in Louisiana. There were 5 soldiers and their wives in that house. The owners and the in-laws each had a room as we each did. We were not used to fancy living. On the farm we had no running water or electric lights. There was a bulb hanging from the ceiling that we plugged everything into. I washed in the bath tub. Appliances were hard to buy because none were being made during the war. I found and electric iron secondhand from somewhere. It had no shutoff. When it got to hot, you unplugged it from the ceiling socket. I made many good friends in that house. There were 14 people living there. On girl got up at 5 am and she was the only one who got a bath every day. Each room had a little gas burner. Most of them leaked and hissed all night. It was a warm climate, but very damp. There was one bathroom. The guys didn't get in every night. I took the bus downtown to eat one meal. I soon couldn't eat the Louisiana fare. It was so spicy and had a lot of cornmeal. I boiled food in the popcorn popper, fried things on a coffee pot burner all plugged into the socket from the ceiling, one at a time. I was happy to be there.

At this point Gerald said he might stay in the army after the war was over. We went to the officer's clubs. We were not allowed to go to the USO's that enlisted men went to. Nobody drank much in those days. We were all young folks away from home. *Rum and Coke* [xxxvii] was the thing to have if you went to the clubs. We met a lot of good people from all over the country. The people from the south were so friendly that you knew them from the northerners. We learned that here was a difference in the thinking of the north and the south. The *Civil War* [xxxviii] was long gone to us, but brought back vividly when you talked to the people from the

South. You learned not to bring the subject up. We had no idea
that it was a problem.

We had a nice Christmas in Louisiana. We bought each
everything we could think of. We spent the day in our room after
we went to church. Some of the girls spent the day crying in their
rooms because their husbands didn't get home. People at home
felt bad because we were away from home, but we didn't mind at
all. They sent goodies, but they didn't stand the mails very well.
We had a bakery just a block from our room where we could buy
all kinds of goodies. At Easter we went to an outside mass on a
hillside. They wore much different clothes than we did at Easter.
It was summer there by then.

This couldn't last forever. The time must come when we must go.
Gerald was out in field for a few days. He wrote me a letter telling
me that he had gotten his orders overseas. It was a hard blow even
thou we knew it was coming. We were getting news all the time of
some of the guys that were killed in action or missing. It wasn't
something to look forward to. When he came in, he was all gung-
ho. He was trained now and he was ready to take his place. We
got ready right away and left for St. Louis. He would take the train
there for New Jersey where he would get on a troop ship to
England. I would take the car and go home. He never said at that
time that he hated to go. We had 3 good days left in St. Louis and
it was the last time I ever saw him. The Mississippi river was
flooding just outside of St. Louis.

Gerald called the highway patrol and asked if the road was open to
Burlington. He was told to go that day before it flooded over. I
was to go to Burlington to my aunt and uncles house and stay the
night. I would take the next day to get to Cresco. The road all
that day was just a path between waterways. One bridge had water
up to the bottom of the bridge. I never knew when it would be all
water.

The next time I heard from Gerald he said, "It is six weeks since I
heard from you and I didn't know if you made it through the
flood." I didn't know where he was. D-Day came and I imagined

him crossing the English Channel. I got a few letters that told me he had gone to France after D-Day

We went to novenas at church every week. Everyone was praying for the men at war. The news didn't come good. We now knew why they needed so many lieutenants. The infantry lieutenants led the troops to the front line on foot. Gerald went with 55 replacements for the front. It was not a good spot to be in. We wrote every day. Sometimes you got bundles of letters bunched. Sometimes you didn't hear anything for a long time.

I had a big map in my bedroom. I put pins where the different divisions were. We watched the news and we waited. I was 3 months pregnant when I went home. I sold the car when I got home. Wives didn't have cars. I got $500 for it. My dad was on the road every day with his car. My mother and I were on the farm. We didn't get any place until he got home.

For our first anniversary he wrote a poem. He wrote it in a foxhole in pencil on lined paper. It was all he could send. Letters were censored and replaced on thing paper to reduce the mail. On July 29, 1944 I got a letter from a 2nd lieutenant who wrote that he and Gerald had promised each other that they would write to their wives if anything happened. He said that Gerald had gone down in front to lead his troops. He and the captain both hit and didn't get back. They were in the hedgerows in France. There were snipers hiding in the *hedgerows* [xxix] that picked off the officers. In a few days a man from the telegram office came to our house with the telegram saying, "We regret to inform you the your husband Gerald Regan is missing in action.

MARY CARROLL

TO MY WIFE ON OUR FIRST ANNIVERSARY
Gerald Regan, July 1944

Though the distance between us is great
 And the miles both long and deep
I'm with you constantly, Mary
 Even though you're lying asleep.

We've spent months together, dear
 And dreamed of a future bright
I live those months in memory again
 Staring sleepless into the night

Where once your head lay on my shoulder
 Is now just an empty space.
I cannot feel your soft hair
 Or touch with my lips, your face.

For now our trail was divided
 No longer we walk hand in hand
You in the good old USA
 And I, in a foreign land

You sleep in your bed 'neath blankets
 While I have a bed on the ground
I'll not complain of my lot
 If only I return safe and sound

A year ago a happy bride,
 Today you're a lonesome wife.
Next year we'll be together
 Forgotten all war and strife

Someday I'll come back to you, Mary
 To you and a little lad,
Who has the blonde curls of his mother
 Or maybe, dark waves like his dad

Or perhaps a little daughter,
 Just the image of the one I love.
What greater blessing could I ask
 Of the one who reigns above?

As I look at the ring on my finger
 I dream of its twin which you wear.
It means a lot to us today,
 Binds for e're and e're.

Yes, I have been true to you, Mary
 True to the vows we both spoke.
With God's help I'll remain,
 True as the heart of an oak.

I long for you beside me
 I miss the touch of your hand
As I lie down to sleep,
 All alone in this foreign land.

Some day this war will be over,
 To you, no more will I write,
For I will be right there with you
 Just as sure as day brings the light.

May July 17th find you happy
 As an angel like you should be.
May God in his mercy, protect you
 And keep you, beloved for me.

As another anniversary rolls around
 May we two to-gether celebrate.
Gone all memories of battle,
 Of fighting, of blood-shed and hate

MARY CARROLL

The bottom had fallen out of my world. Nobody came, nothing happened. It was just over. It was our duty to tell his family. It was very difficult. I was within 3 months of having a baby. My dad went to the telegraph office and told them that if anything else came, he would pick it up and not to deliver it. I soon knew that Dad knew he was dead. One day the Regans were at our place and Mr. (Johnny) Regan said," I'm sure that one of these days we'll hear from him." Dad said," I hope so," and he was crying. I didn't ask him then because I knew they wouldn't tell me before my baby was born. I guess I didn't want to know.

On October 17th at midnight in 1944, I went to the hospital with the most awful pains that I had ever had. The nurses sent the folks home and told them they would call them when something happened. I spent the rest of the night in the delivery room by myself, knowing nothing about what should be happening. The nurses were in and out. At 7am they took me out and put another mother in. When they finished, the Dr. came to see me. They put me back into the delivery room and the Dr. said, "Give her ether and we'll take it with forceps. This has gone on long enough." I had a beautiful baby boy in the morning.

When my Dad came in I said, "You know he is dead, don't you?" He started to cry and I knew it was true. The Dr. came in and said, "You're not telling her now, are you?" I said, "They didn't have to, I knew."

I thought that Gerald would have been so proud. There was no funeral, no nothing. It was all over. People were very kind. We had a memorial mass in the Elma church then. And now my life was different.

It was a long cold winter that year. Most of the girls that I knew were with their husbands or working at some war work. I didn't have a car, but I didn't think I had any place to go anyway. I was at Elma when the war was declared over. I was in the Regan yard when the bells in town started to ring. Then the fire whistle blew. It was a happy day when the war was over, but it had lost its joy for me. The cars started streaming by. We didn't go to the

celebration. As time went on the boys started coming home.
There was no big celebration. I guess everyone was involved and
there was none left to cheer.

It wasn't all a happy ending. The soldiers were to have their jobs
back and have a wage until they got situated. Some couldn't settle
down. There were a lot of nerves shot and wounds in many ways.
Some wives and girlfriends didn't wait. Some sent money home
and it was not there. Some had been in lonely spots, such as on
islands, and had spent free time drinking. There were many habits
to change. Some of the children didn't know their fathers. The
VFW clubs didn't help. They were for men only and the fellows
spent their time and money there. A lot of homes were broken.
Some soldiers couldn't stop talking about what had happened to
them. Some couldn't talk about it at all. I realized that I didn't
have all the problems.

Four years later in 1948, we were given the choice to bring the
bodies of fallen soldiers back or leave them where they were. It
seemed a sense of finish to bring them back. I wanted to have a
funeral for Gerald in Cresco. That was where Danny and I lived.
It was where Danny's friends would realize why he didn't have a
father. The stores would close for the time of the funeral and the
flags would fly at half mast. The Regans and I met at the funeral
home to make plans. The memorial mass had been in Elma. I
was the next of kin and I had the choice. I told Mr. Regan I
wanted the funeral in Cresco and I would compromise and bury
him in Elma. He got very upset. Funerals were to be from the
home where the body would be taken and the people would show
their respect by staying with the body night and day until it was
buried. "Nobody was to take him in to a cold old funeral parlor
and leave him there." As I continued to make the plans Mr.
Regan got up going out slamming the door. I went on with my
plans and Mrs. Regan said, "Lets don't let this break any ties with
us."

The body came in on the train to Cresco. The legion met it with
the flags flying. Danny was 4 years old and I wanted this to be
something he and his friends would remember. We had one night

wake at the funeral parlor. Mr. and Mrs. Regan stayed up all night with the body. I told them I couldn't because I had a child at home and couldn't get through the next day if I did. The Cresco Legion followed the body to Elma and when we got there the Elma Legion formed a guard under which the hearse was taken. When we got back to Cresco, the VFW ladies had dinner ready at my house. This laid matters to rest. We could go on with our lives.

I loved him dearly and never forgot him, but I could do no more. I've wondered all these years if he's up there waiting for me. The following is the poem that Gerald wrote for our first anniversary. I had it printed and framed after he died. I didn't receive it until I got the notice he was missing. Many, many letters came back to me then marked "deceased." I saved these letters and mementos for years, but the years went on, I couldn't bear to read them over and over.

RITA SHEA

In the summer of 1946, Danny and I were living with my folks in their house on 6th Ave in Cresco, Iowa. Dan was 2 years old. His dad, Gerald Regan, had been killed in the battles of France. One afternoon Rita Shea came to our back door with a paper sack filled with her belongings. "Can I come and live with you?" she asked. Some of the girls that I knew who worked downtown had been talking about Rita. Rita had been adopted by Bill and Mayme Shea when she was a year old. Mayme was now dead and Bill was very old. The authorities had placed her in many homes as a foster child. She would not stay with any of them. They had been old people and she didn't feel at home with them. My friends said that it was said that it would be necessary to send her to the Good Shepherd Home in Dubuque. That was a home for wayward girls. Most of them were unwed mothers. We all agreed that this was not the place for Rita. They didn't feel that she should go there unless she was in trouble. She had been staying with the family next door us. Things were not going well there. She came in and started school from our house.

It seemed logical to me that she and her dad could make it by themselves. Rita and I arranged to meet her Dad and her "cousin" Marie who wanted Bill to live with her. We met in her car downtown. Rita asked her dad to rent an apartment with her so they could have a home. He really wasn't able to look after her so he didn't say much. Cousin Marie would have none of it. I want Uncle Bill to live with me." she said. Rita expected she wanted Bill to be her chore boy on the farm and have his $50/MO, pension check. I said, "If you do that, what will happen to Rita?"

She said, "She isn't related to me. I will take care of Uncle Bill, but I don't care what happens to her." I asked Bill if he cared if we looked for her real mother. He said he didn't care if we looked for her, but he wouldn't sign her away as long as he was alive.

When we got home the man in charge, Mr. Lomas called us. Rita was now a ward of the state. We never knew how he knew what was going on. From then on he knew everything we did. He said, "I'll give you $50/month if you'll keep her." I hadn't realized there was any money involved. I said I'd keep her. I was getting a total of $130/month at the time. I got $50 a month pension for myself and $25/month for Danny. We also were getting $55/month from government insurance. With another $50 a month we could have a home of our own. We went downtown then and bought Rita a coat and a pair of shoes. The coat was one of those with a fish tail back that were popular at the time. It was a loud plaid. I wonder why we liked it.

Rita started school and soon the lost look left her face. She got to be friends of the girls and she didn't feel so left out. Her classmates started to come to the house and she was a part of her class.

We started to look for an apartment. My mother didn't want us to leave. She didn't want us to leave since Danny was born. She said, "You can't take him away from us now." I knew we couldn't all stay there. We found a 2 room apartment and told my mother after we had rented it. She cried and made us feel awful. It was a kitchen and a living room and a back porch. We bought a washing machine, sofabed, table and chairs and a gas cook stove. Danny and I slept in the living room. He had a baby bed and I had the sofa. Rita had my grandmothers iron single bed on the back porch. I don't know what we planned to do about her sleeping on the porch when it got cold. We were real happy there. We paid $15 a month for it. We never thought it was small. We didn't have a car. Rita walked to the show, roller skating and to the cafe for a pop with the girls. We shared a bathroom and an ice box.

When fall came we found a four room upstairs apartment. It had a living room kitchen and two bedrooms. The bathroom was a stool in a closet. We had no hot water. The land lady said that she had washed her feet in the kitchen sink for many years so that's the way we did it too. Our telephone was a big brown box on the wall. I bought twin beds for Danny and I in one bedroom. Rita had the back bedroom. We had two oil stoves to keep us warm. Rita had one in her bedroom. We both carried our oil up the back winding stairs every night. One stove in the kitchen heated the other rooms. We like it there.

Rita did part time work at the Elms Cafe where her mother worked when she was alive. She always made her own spending money. I don't remember giving her money. I got a job doing the book work for a furniture store. I went every morning except Saturday and Sunday until I got the books balanced for the day. I usually worked an hour a day. At the month end, I spent a few days. I walked Danny to my mothers where he stayed while I worked. I got a $/hr. This was the most I had ever earned and much more than most of the girls downtown got. We thought it was because my boss came from a bigger city where people got that. That gave us another $25/month. Christmas these years were very hard for Rita. We would always go to my folks for Christmas where some of the rest of my family would join us. Most of these days Rita spent upstairs laying on her face crying. All she would say was' "they are not my family."

It was a while we were in the upstairs apartment that we decided to find Rita's mother. I never considered what I would be like if she found her and went to live with her. We were a family now. It seemed a lonely little girl should find her mother if she had one. She had a baptism certificate that her folks had gotten when she made her first communion. Rita had a friend, Mary Ann who was adopted in Cresco about the same time. They told who the mothers were. The mothers were sponsors for the others baby. Mary Ann had an idea who her mother was because this women would come to visit her occasionally. Rita knew that her mother was Marie Billmeyer and that she was placed in the baby-fold in Dubuque. Mary Ann asked her mother who Marie Billmeyer had married and was told that it was Milton Viverburg. We only had to find Milton Viverburg. Rite's class went to Dubuque for a class trip. She got Father Sewn to go to the courthouse there to find some information. They found nothing.

Rita wrote to the postmaster in Dubuque and asked him to send her M. Viverburg's address. The postmaster was not allowed to give out addresses, but it happened that he knew the people. He

gave them a call. Her mother had given her the name Rita Mae
before she left her. When they learned that a Rita Mae was
looking for them, they knew who it would be. Milton worked for
the railroad and so they got on the train and came to Cresco.

  They had looked for her for years and the home wouldn't tell
them where she was. We had written the orphanage and told
them that Rita needed a home and that we would like to find her
mother. They told us that her mother had married and that her
new family knew nothing about her and they could do nothing.

Mr. Shea was 85 years old now and in the hospital and very sick.
Rita spent every moment she could with him until he died. It was
on the day of the funeral that the Viverburgs came to Cresco.
After the funeral, Rita went to a friend's house and I went back to
work. They were a little afraid that if the people who had adopted
Rita knew nothing of this they wouldn't be welcome.

When the Viverburgs arrived in Cresco, they asked where they
could find Rita Shea. They were directed to call me at the
furniture store. It seemed a strange call for her to get on the day of
her father's funeral. I told him I couldn't tell him where she was
unless he told me who he was. He was cautious because they
didn't know if they would be welcome. Finally he said, "my name
is Viverburg." I said, " Is our wife with you?" He knew then that I
knew who they were. I told them to come to the store and we
would get Rita. I gave her a call and asked Rita to meet me at our
apartment. When Marie walked in the store I knew that she was
Rita's mother because she look like her. It was a grand reunion
when we got to the apartment. They both knew who the other was
when they met. Marie told of how she and her husband went back
to the orphanage every year on her birthday to see if they would
tell where she was. They were all sworn to secrecy at the
orphanage and nobody would tell. Marie cried and cried when
she told us she stayed at the home for a year and worked rather
than sign the papers to give the baby away. She would soon be too
big for the *babyfold*[xl] and would have to go to a different place
and they talked her into signing. In a few years she was married to
Milton and by then they wouldn't tell where Rita was.

Rita told me later that she went into her back bedroom and cried that day. She said that somehow she felt that when she found her mother she would have Mom Shea back and that didn't happen.

Rita packed a few of her belongings and returned to Dubuque with them. I don't think she went with the intention of staying. Rita was just settled into our little apartment and she was happy there. Dubuque was big to her. She was pretty independent and could go anywhere in Cresco by herself. She could walk to all her activities. In Dubuque she had to be taken and waited for. There were 3 more children in their home and she had to share a room with 2 half sisters.

 In a week I got a call that she wanted to share a room with 2 half sisters. The next week I got a call that she wanted to come home and would I meet the bus. She did eventually go back and see them a few times, but she would never stay. Her half brother would come and see her in later years. She became friends with her two sisters too.

I don't know how the authorities always knew what we were doing. Father Sweeney came to see me while she was gone to be sure that she had a home when she came back. I don't think I ever considered that she would not come back. I didn't want to lose her then. Mr. Lomas said, "I told you to leave that alone. I have seen those cases and they are not all happy ones." One summer Rita got a job at the Deerwood which was a nightclub. I never gave it a thought that she was a minor. It wasn't long before Mr. L called and said, "Get her out of there."

Rita had an Uncle Mike. He was Mom Shea's brother. He was old and in the hospital. Rita went up there and stayed with him when she wasn't in school.

Cousin Marie got wind that she was spending time with him. She started to be there when Rita was. It seems that he had a little money. Money didn't enter into our lives because we didn't have very much and we didn't consider it. I don't know if they changed his will or not.

On Rita's wedding day she got a letter saying she would get her Mothers share which was $240. Rita was happy because it would buy her a refrigerator. In later years Marie's brothers treated her in the same way. She wanted to have a place to stay while she met Allen's boat when he was in the Navy. Their message was "You were adopted. You are not related to me." I don't think she ever met these cousins who were related to the Sheas.

When Danny was five years old, my grandmother's house became available to us. My dad rented it to us for $35/month. We had a kitchen, two bedrooms, dining room and a living room. We had a coal furnace and could wash in the basement. We had hot water. By this time I was working in the furniture store more hours and we bought furniture that we needed. You could not buy a refrigerator during the war. Now you put your name on a list and you got one when one came up. You pretty much took what came into the store. We got rid of our ice-box and got a refrigerator. I watched a pop-up toaster on the counter where I worked for a long time before I felt I could afford it. It was a real treat because it tasted so different from what we had. The 45 RPM single-records just came in then and we had to have a player for them. It plugged into a radio.
Danny was just a block from kindergarten. Rita was 3 blocks from school and we were two blocks from downtown. We really enjoyed our new home. Rita brought her friends from school here. Some of the girls that I knew that worked downtown had just sleeping rooms or lived at home. This gave them a place to spend time at our house. Rita was working at the Elms Cafe after school.

I had a plain blue rug in the living room. One day I spent a long time shampooing it. That night Rita came home with some of her friends. It was raining. They walked one fella around and around the house. They told me they couldn't let him go home because they didn't want his folks to know that he had too much to drink.

This was new to us. I shampooed the rug over again the next day to get the mud out. One night I volunteered to take Rita's class to Decorah to say the rosary over the radio. After we were through, I took them to the Legion Club for a treat. Liquor was allowed in private clubs at the time. People who wanted a mixed drink had to take a bottle with them and keep it under the table after they had mixed it with their pop.

When I got in there I realized what I had done. The barkeeper said, "What are you doing with that bunch of kids in here? That's how simple we were about the drinking world.

There was one friend of mine that Rita didn't like, named Burnie. Rita told her off one day when she tried to tell her what to do. "And furthermore, you can quit telling Mary what to do, too." Rita said. We had a good time in our little house. It was home to us. We didn't go very far nor did we spend much money. Our first Christmas there, we had a big tree in the big south windows. Danny got an electric train that year. Rita was not so concerned about being alone for Christmas that time.

Around prom time Rita was in a store looking at prom dresses with some friends. Rita put one on, but she knew she couldn't have the money for it. The lady waited on her told her to come back the nest day after school. The clerk was the wife of Mr. L. who took care of her affairs. She told Rita she could have the dress and told her that Mr. L. said it was all right. She was very proud of that dress. She got the lead in the operetta that year and she had something to wear when she sang the solo. She did a beautiful job and she looked wonderful in her prom dress. I was congratulated that night as if she was my daughter and I was pretty proud.

All of the girls who graduated that year were getting cedar chests from our store. I decided my girl should have one too. I didn't buy many things for her. She was very proud of the cedar chest. I think she still has it.

Rita went back to work at the *fountain* [xi] of the drug store after she graduated. She still lived with us. She kept connections with her mother but never went to stay with them again. While Rita was a senior in high school, she went to her friend Patty's house one day.

Patty's cousin was visiting. His name was Allan Bruce and he was home from the Navy. He looked pretty nifty in his white sailor suit. Rita lost her heart that day. She never had eyes for anyone else after that. After that she knew what she wanted to do. Mr. L wanted to help her go to Beauty school, but she'd had enough of school.

When Rita and Allan decided to get married that September, Rita had money enough to buy her own wedding dress. She picked a dainty inexpensive one and looked lovely.

We decided that we should have her wedding dinner at our house. Catholic weddings were all in the morning at that time. That way we had to have a lunch at noon. We didn't have too many to invite. We had Allan's immediate family, Rita's mother, stepfather and her half sisters and brother. A few of her friends were there and Father Carpenter. We borrowed two folding tables from the store where I worked. We had 25 people. We fussed over the table and had goblets.

We hired a lady to cook the dinner and make a wedding cake. We really worked to have it as dainty and it was as lovely as we thought it would be. When the people sat down the room was full. We had no way to serve food. We were embarrassed. They had to take the food through the bedroom and around. I breathed a sigh of relief and said my part was done.

What a surprise I got when we got to Elma. His family was going to have a little reception before the dance in the evening. There were about 150 people there. The tables were filled with platters of fried chicken, ham, salads, fresh rolls...... there was a table of cakes of every kind; angel food, devil's food, and other pretty treats. A lot of the neighbor ladies were there to serve it. We didn't have neighbors like that. Our part looked small-- and we did so much worrying.

There was a dance in the *hall*[xlii] that night. Mr. and Mrs. Viverburg danced that night and really had a good time. Rita fit right in and you'd think she'd always had a big family.

I went home that night feeling that I had a job well done. I figured that she was in good hands and that they would accept her as one of their big family. I knew then that Rita would never lay on her face on Christmas again and say, "They don't belong to me!"

MARY CARROLL

WEBERS

After Rita left there was a gap in our house. It seemed logical to fill that gap. As we were close to a school, I rented a room to a teacher. We could use the income, too. A teacher named Marcia Hartwig came into the lives of Danny and I. Marcia was a very interesting person. She came from North Dakota. She was quite popular with the teachers and the young blades in town. She stayed two years with us. Leaving some broken hearts behind, she went back home to marry her hometown sweetheart. She was surprised about all the trees in Iowa and the leaves that were to be raked up in the fall. We had a lot of good times together. While she was there I decided to buy a car. Not many ladies had their own car in those days. It was a 51 Plymouth. It cost me $2000 new. We had many good times going to the night spots of the day. Many clubs opened up after the war. I was eligible to belong to the Legion and WFW clubs. They had dances and parties. A lot of the working girls from around town spent time at my house. They were living at home and it was more fun to be on their own with us. We had some real good times.

I was about 30 years old. In those days there were very few single people about. Some of those I went with were younger. There were not many free men about. They all married the one waiting for them during the war. There was Clarence from Decorah who couldn't see marrying a Catholic. There was Lyle from Postville who couldn't raise someone else's child. There was Don who couldn't leave his mother.

One Sat afternoon, I decided that Danny and I would go to Elma and spend the night with Grandpa and Grandma Regan. As we drove into Elma, we met a car with Gerald's sister Kathleen and her boyfriend Harold Theile and Al Weber. It was the coldest and stormiest day of the winter. Al and Harold stopped us and asked me to go to Charles City with them. Kathleen had been wanting me to meet Al for some time. We took Danny to the Regan's house and I left my car there. That was my first date with Al Weber. We started going together from then on. Harold and Kathleen were married the following January.

The Webers lived in Stacyville, IA. When Al was old enough to go to high school, his family moved to a farm near Elma. It was next to the country church at St. Cecelia. Al had made plans to stay in Stacyville and go to high school. He was going to go to stay with his brother Gilbert on the farm and do chores for his room and board. That year he became very ill with *rheumatic fever*[xliii]. Instead of going to school he spent nearly a year in bed. This disease was very damaging to the valves in his heart. They didn't have *antibiotics*[xliv] to kill infection in those days. Al was not well from that time on. He worked for his dad for a few years on the farm. He worked for his brother Ves for a while. When he was old enough he went to Waterloo to work in a packing plant. To start, he was put in the hog slaughtering division. When he became sick they sent him home. He was so sick he went to his rooms and stayed until one of his friends found him and took him to Elma.

The Doctor in Elma said he knew what it was, but he didn't know how to treat it. He went to the Stacyville doctor who Al always said saved his life. It was *Malta fever*[xlv]. It is sometimes called brucellosis. At that time not much was known about it. It had malaria symptoms, fevers, chills, and aches in the bones. This disease was to stay with him all the rest of his life and caused him much suffering. It was a long time before he could work again.

When I met him he was ready to go back to work and was looking for a job. A fellow from Elma that he knew was working as a meat cutter in a store in Marshalltown. He got him a job there cutting meat. It was a training job where he would get more wages after he learned the trade. He got $45/week. He was real pleased with it and liked the town. We didn't get to see each other very often after he went to Marshalltown. Al would come to Cresco on the weekends. On a couple of weekends, Danny and I went to Marshalltown and stayed in the hotel. Once in a while we would meet half way. I was working at the *furniture store*^{xlvi}. My boss sold out. The new owner didn't keep the same help and we all lost our jobs. I was out of work and the winter was coming on. We decided we should be together instead of all that driving.

On Nov. 8th, 1952, we were married in Cresco. Friends of mine said they would put on a reception for us. We were married in the morning as all Catholics were then. We had a dinner for the immediate families downtown in a cafe. We took a trip through Wisconsin and Illinois and back to Marshalltown to the house we had rented. We had a nice 4 room Cape Cod house and we moved in before Thanksgiving.

 Much to our dismay, the landlord only wanted someone for the winter. On the first of March we had to find a different place to live. We rented a nice downstairs apartment. We had a very nice couple who lived upstairs who we spent much time with. In September we had a lovely girl. I had been raised with boys and I welcomed a sweet little baby girl.

We weren't there very long when Al was told he would be asked to go to the Clifton store in Tama. We told our landlord this and before the job came up he had rented the apartment. We moved again. This time to a house that a deaf lady lived in. She kept the upstairs and we had 4 rooms downstairs. We got along with her very well. Of course the time came for us to go to Tama. We didn't find a house right away, so Al drove back and forth all winter. He wasn't real happy with the Tama situation. He expected to be the manager of the meat department there. We moved to a big old house in Tama and Danny started school there. He was in the 4th grade. We spent a year in Tama. The town was old, dirty, and rough. There was an *Indian settlement* ^{xlvii} about 5 miles from town. There was a lot of unemployment and poverty. It had been a railroad town and the railroad had moved on. It was nothing to have a bum at your back door asking for food. We always fed them. We'd make a sandwich and coffee and pass it out to the porch. They never made trouble. The Indians were not employed much of the time. Some went to the factories in Cedar Rapids, but not all. Danny found the kids kind of tough and he had to fight his way many a time.

On March 4, 1954 we were watching the evening news and saw one street in Elma in flames. Al was quite excited and called his brother there. That weekend we went to Elma. One block of the town stores had burned down. We talked to one party who would build a bowling alley if he could get someone to rent the top story for a store. As Al was dissatisfied with his job and Tama, it seemed like a good idea. The clothing store had burned down so we thought there was a need for another one. We went back to Tama with the plan to move to Elma and start a clothing store. We had $4000. We really had no idea what we were getting into. In August, the man said that if we could come to Elma before he got the building built, he would give Al a job helping with that. In Aug. we packed our things again and started for Elma. It was midnight when we got the truck into Elma. I was driving our car with the kids and a load of our belongings. If I could have turned around at that moment, I would have done so. It looked pretty bleak and little at that time of night. The old house we had rented was no prize either.

The old illnesses were coming back on Al. When he carried heavy quarters of beef on his back and went into the freezers he was ill. We thought a clothing store was going to be much easier for him. If he were working on his own he could manage it better. The builder arranged that he take Al's wages out of the rent when he occupied the store. This gave us no income for months. We had had a good life in Marshalltown. I enjoyed the larger stores at Christmas time and the parks in the summertime. A lot of young people worked at Cliftons. They got together for picnics and parties. We helped each other move and had coffee together when the guys had a break.. Al enjoyed the work as long as it was in Marshalltown. He felt he should have been up for manager in

Tama. When the boss brought someone new in to be manager, he lost interest.

Now we were among family. The Webers were many. There were 6 brothers and a sister. They all lived within driving distance for an afternoon. They were kind and got along well. We got along had some good times. They helped each other and lent money as they needed it. You never heard a Weber say a harsh word against his own. They spoke well of the wives and to them. I don't ever remember Al saying a cross word to me. You could figure on some Weber being around on Sundays. When Al was sick they came to see him often. When we went to Ed Weber's on a Sunday, he always had two chickens on the grill. There was always beer. If you went to Kenny's in Dougherty, IA, Eileen had a chicken in the oven and potato salad in the refrigerator. At Gilberts, they always had fried steak. Grandma Weber was famous for her baked beans. Our families were growing to be able to enjoy each other also.

We were living in this old house the winter Creighton was born. The young doctor came to Elma about the time we did. Creighton was the second baby he delivered in Elma. On a cold crisp night we went to New Hampton to the hospital. When morning came and no baby was delivered, Dr. Rainy said to Al, "Your wife will hate me, but I'm going to have to turn the baby." It was a very painful thing, but soon after a precious little boy was born. It was January 7, 1955. Al came to the hospital with the thought of naming him Creighton. There had been a boy in the store that day and his mother had called him "Creighton". Al thought that was the best. Soon after that a lady came to our house and asked us to rent her house.

It was a great improvement over what we had. It had a new automatic oil furnace. That was the first heat that we had had that we didn't have to stoke in the coal. That was the house by the Elma park. It stands today, but it doesn't look like it did when we live in it. It was a nice home with plenty of room and It had just been redecorated.

Or store went very well in the beginning. The town needed the place to buy a lot of the things that we had. Pheasant season in the fall was always good for lots of business. The town was full of hunters. We always did a good business with boots, gloves and caps. For a few years, our store was just what was needed there. However we didn't realize what was happening in the clothing business elsewhere. Kmart, Pamida, and Farm Fleet were going into the larger towns. We could no longer compete with them in buying. They bought larger quantities and could sell cheaper. It was also happening to the grocery stores. Our friends across the street were having a hard time hanging on to their clothing store.

ELMA

We were having a good time in Elma. We knew everybody. They made their own fun. We had parties, clubs, and lots of card games. We were a part of the business crowd and were in the Commercial Club. We had dinners once a month and the firemen held dances and Halloween parties. There were two schools and there were basketball games, proms, Fourth of July celebrations and lots of other things going on.

When we lived near the park, we had another baby boy. We called him Gary. Al was proud of his growing family and he was good with babies and helped care for them. Gary was a little red-headed boy and so good-natured, he got along with everybody.

After Christmas season of 1957 our business was falling off and we couldn't pay the rent. There was a building uptown for sale. Al thought we could live upstairs and have the clothing store downstairs. We bought it and moved the family upstairs. We would build on when business picked up. We never added on. We moved in March 1958.

In Dec. of '58 Al became very sick. Dr. Rainy sent him to the Mayo clinic with the thought that he had cancer of the lung. They didn't prove that it was cancer, but said that something was there and they had to get it out. It was after Christmas 1958 when they operated and found an "inflammatory thing." After the lab report came back it was determined to be brucellosis. Again it had come back.

The lung operation was a terrible blow to his system. While he was getting better an abscess came in the calf in his leg. In New Hampton Hospital, they removed this and again the infection was the same. Before he got over this another abscess formed on his tailbone. They didn't operate this time, but opened it in the Drs. office. As if that was not enough, one came on the other leg. They drained that and put a tube in it. In all, it was six months before he was able to come down to the store. I worked in the store, Creighton with me.   Al kept Gary upstairs with him.

When summer came, Al got a job selling things to farmers. Al was not the salesman out of the store that he was in his own business. We got along with what the store brought in, but we were getting terribly in debt. In the fall, Al got a job with a carpenter who was building a house out of town. It was cold work and hard on the road with shingling.

The man who operated the state liquor store was dying of cancer. I didn't want him to go after that job. The Webers had liquor when they gathered and I hated to see him so close to it. This was one time he went against me and said, "I'm going to do this whether you support me or not." It was a political job and if you got the right signers from you party, you could get it. Reuben Tuchek was the chairman and they got the signers they needed in Cresco. The next day Harold Showalter took him to Des Moines. There he was sworn in and fingerprinted. Al was very happy with his new business. It was very strictly operated. The state controlled it. The book work was easy for Al. He was inside and feeling quite well.

The clothing store was losing ground. I was operating it. We couldn't get any new stock. Al wouldn't let go of it until all of the companies were paid. I arranged that I paid some each week. This kept them from closing us up. Some I paid as little as $5.00/week. Then Social Security came and made us give them a weekly amount also. In the fall of 1960 we closed the door. It was a sad day. We didn't have enough capital to start or enough know-how and the need was no longer there. Al found a man who bought odd lot merchandise. He came with a truck. We lost money and we both cried that night. It was also a relief. We owed no one and I could go back to raising my family and keeping house. It was a real feeling of failure. Al was now making

$330/month in the liquor store.   He had started at $260. We found someone who wanted to rent our place for a TV repair shop. We found a big old house on the other side of town and made room for all of us. We paid $50 a month and we got the same for our place. We had hopes of selling it to the tenant, but that was not to be. Danny was in college at this time in 1963. The kids were getting bigger and Al was feeling quite well.

This simple life was not to last long. On March 1st I came home from a wedding shower to find Al in his chair unaware of what was going on.. He had taken the car to the other side of town and was sitting in it when somebody he knew found him and brought him home. He had had a heart attack. Dr. Rainy thought best if he went to a specialist. We got him to Mason City to the heart specialist. When I went to see him the Dr. told me, "I can't keep your husband alive." We went to his room and he told Al, "I cannot keep you alive. Dr. Rainy cannot keep you alive. You will never see you young family grown. There is only one chance for you. You can go to Iowa City. They are replacing heart valves there. It is a new operation. They will put a plastic valve in your heart to replace the one damaged by rheumatic fever you had as a young man. It is the only chance you have." The operation was only 2 years old.

Al didn't want to go to Iowa City. The lung operation was so terrible that he couldn't think of doing it again. I talked him into it. He had to go to Iowa City for test and when he came back he had lost about 10 years. He was all in from the blood tests. On May 20th 1964, they operated on his heart. I didn't have a car good enough to get me to the hospital. I took the bus. Eileen Weber called and said, "I won't let you go there alone. I'll be on the bus when you get to Charles City and I'll go with you.

   Danny was in *College*[xlviii] in Illinois. He came to be with us. Eileen stayed as long as she could. Danny and I could not all stay overnight in the room with Al. Al was in intensive care and we could only go in every hour for 5 minutes. We rented a room. I slept in it at night and Danny stayed at the hospital all night. I stayed at the hospital in the day and Danny slept.

Danny was graduating from his college courses that week but he didn't get to go to the graduation. He started out once toward St. Bede's, but came back. He said, "I can't leave you alone." It was nine days before Al came to. When he came to his mind was very mixed up. One Dr. told us he had brain damage because his heart stopped on the *operating table*[xlix]. Other Drs. wouldn't give us any satisfaction about it. We tried to believe that some of it was the medications. My brother Jerry came to be with us for a while. He left me some money to get me through. My dad also sent me money. I stayed as long as I could. My kids were at the neighbors and at Ves Webers. Al was there 30 days.

He had three months sick leave and pay. The time was running out and so was my money. He seemed to recover when he got home, but there was still the possibility of brain damage. He would go to the faucet with a glass and not know how to get a drink. He would go to the door and not know how to get it open.

Danny and Joyce were getting married on Labor Day weekend 1964.

As his brother Kenny told him, "Al, You wouldn't look so sick if you had clothes to fit you." We needed to get him a suit to wear to the wedding. I drove to Mason City and put a suit on my Sears charge card. He was so sick he couldn't stand up in the store while they fitted the suit. We went to Danny's wedding, but it was all he could do. His new suit was soaking with sweat.

We had to go to New Hampton every week to test his blood. Sometimes it was so low we had to leave him there. In all, he was in the hospital 16 times in 5 years. He tried to go back to work, but the auditor came and sent him home. He was not able to work again. This was the last of his hopes.

I called the Dr. every night before he went to sleep to get a shot of morphine. Dr. said, "I'd give him all he wants if I could." Al walked the floor until the Dr. got there, his fists clenched with the pain.

Two weeks after the wedding, I called Dr. Rainy at 3 AM. He said to get the ambulance. We took Al to the hospital. The nurse kept telling me to get someone to stay with me, but I had seen him so sick so many times before, I waited until I didn't have to wake anyone and called his brother Ves. As soon as Ves got there Al told him, "I'm not going to make it this time." He died at 8 AM. How I hated to go back and tell those 3 little kids he was gone. Before the fall was over we also buried Ves' wife and their father, Grandpa Weber. It had a startling effect on us all. Al was just 40 years old. It was Sept. 22nd, 1964.

MARY CARROLL

The Next Chapter

When Al died, I was 46 years old. Gary was 7, Creighton was 9 an Colleen 11. Danny, 20, was married and living in Minneapolis with Joyce. We were living in a big house on the east side of Elma. Al had 3 month of sick pay coming but that soon ran out. He had enough insurance proceeds to pay the bills and the funeral expenses. Sadly six weeks later our dear friend Lois Weber passed away with cancer. We had spent a lot of time with Lois' family since we'd moved to Elma. We tried to do things with other cousins but there were often six or more children of all different ages. Grandpa Weber died just 3 months later. These deaths stayed with the Weber family for a long time.

The big house that we were renting was sold so we had to move again. On New Year's Day, Danny and some of his friends moved us to a house near the school in Elma. It wasn't a very desirable place. I paid $40 a month. It was a big, drafty two storey house that needed space heaters in the rooms upstairs. We all moved downstairs and we were still cold.

When summer came I started thinking of ways to stay warm and make a living. I had the building downtown which had been the clothing store, which had living rooms upstairs. I went to Des Moines to see if I could take the job at the liquor store that Al had done. They told me that they didn't hire women. Later I went to Charles City to take a test with Sears. The man told me that I had passed very well but that I was too old to be put on the Sears retirement plan. Next I took a test in New Hampton for a telephone company job. The man who gave the test chose me for the job but his boss wanted a local girl that he knew. Some ladies and I went back to New Hampton and took nurses training at the hospital. At this time I was getting $55.00 for each of the four of us per month from Social Security, but if I went back to work I would lose my part of the check.

I had to find something to supplement my income to have enough to live on. I did some substitute work at the library that summer, making $1/hr. I made enough money to buy the school books for the fall. Since I had the nurses' aid training I decided to finish the downstairs of my building for a place to take in old people. There were no rest homes nearby. One of Danny's friends made a sign for me, which said, "Merirest". I had a new furnace in the building and we would be warm there.

I had new sheetrock, flooring and a bathroom put in. Quite quickly I had two patients. One was 90 years old and the other was in a wheelchair, which required 24-hr duties. However I discovered that I couldn't do it alone. One patient paid me $150/mo. and the other paid $100/mo., paid by the county. I couldn't hire help at that rate though. Shortly the 90 year old had a stroke and the one in the wheel chair broke her hip. They both went to state sponsored assisted living facilities.

My mother Mae Ahern became very ill about this time. She and my dad, Emmitt Carroll, moved into my rest home. Mom soon slipped into a coma. Dad helped me with her. Six weeks later she died. Dad said, "I'm going to stay." He rented their home in Cresco and divided their furniture among the Carroll children. Dad's coming helped me a lot. He paid his way and helped me by staying with the kids once in a while. He was with us for 8 years.

One evening, two years after Al died, I was going to the grocery store when a man came up to my car. He asked me to go to the bingo game with him the next night. I knew him because he had come into the old store. This was Joe Mulick. He and his dad farmed west of Elma. His dad had died a couple of years earlier. He told Harold Showalter that he could no longer stay on the farm alone. Harold told him to try to come and see me. Harold was always a good friend of the family. Joe and I started going together then. Joe was 50 years old and I was 48. We decided that in the spring we would get married. We wanted to do it quietly. We were married on April 4, 1968. We were only going to have Joe's sister and her husband there to stand up for us but Danny, Joyce and the kids were all there too. Somehow Danny and Joyce and the Showalters had figured out the time and surprised us. We were married at 5 in the morning! Dan and Joyce came the night before and stayed with her folks. They were all back to work the next day. Joe and I left right away for the Ozark mountains in Missouri. Neither of us had been to the Ozarks but we needed to get away and it was a great vacation.

By this time Colleen was 14, Creighton 12 and Gary was 10. Joe was still farming. When school was out that summer, the kids would all go to the farm and help with haying and other chores. Colleen drove the tractor and I took meals for them and for the other men who helped them. By that fall Joe had decided that he was tired of farming and that farming from town was particularly difficult. So on the coldest day in December he had a farm sale. He sold the equipment, the animals and the farm.

Joe and I both looked for work that winter. We went to the canning factory in Blue Earth, MN, the trailer factory in Forest City and a small factory in Waukon. One after another we were told that we would not be hired because of our ages. But when I applied for a job at a clothing store in Osage, they hired me. Joe didn't find a job in Osage but a friend asked him to come and work at the Equity Co-op in Elma. He worked there for 12 years until he was 62. He liked the work and he liked the people around him that he knew.

For a while I was able to substitute teach, as I had done so many years teaching in the country schools. Later I went to the home for mentally handicapped children, which begun at the convent of the Catholic parish when the elementary school was closed. We had about a dozen young people there at any one time. I arrived at 6:30am and got breakfast and packed lunches, for them to take to the workshops. The old gym was used for the workshops. I made $25.00/day teaching and $2.60/hr at the home. That was the highest wage I ever made.

All the time our kids were growing our little town of Elma was becoming less attractive. The schools were closed. A lot of the businesses were gone. The children all rode the school bus 25 miles to Cresco. With a new dad and a distant school, these were hard days for kids growing up.

Gary was still at home when Dad got sick. One Friday night, Dad couldn't talk and by the time Jerry and Kay got there, he went into a coma. On Monday morning early, he passed away. The kids got used to grandpa being a part of our family. Now they had another funeral to get used to.

They each worked at the Dan Conway grocery store as soon as they were old enough. This took their time after school and on Saturdays. Sports and band were in Cresco. The boys were in Little League some but it was Colleen who really followed ball playing. She had a coach who took them to other towns for games. The boys had paper routes. Together they delivered the papers for 10 years. They were not allowed to drive Joe's car so they didn't learn to drive until they had they had their own cars. Each helped the other learn with their car. They developed some good friends with whom they went to college. They depended on each other and Danny was their mentor in many ways. This helped me too.

Colleen went off to junior college in Mason City. She drove an old car and worked at the drive-in theater out in the country. Sometimes that car got her there and sometimes it didn't. With two other Elma girls, Colleen stayed her first year at the YWCA in Mason City. Creighton left the next year with Dad's old car, a Studebaker Lark. He went to Iowa State University at Ames, Iowa. He worked several jobs there. One time he worked at the cafeteria for his meals and one time for a t-shirt company. Three years later Gary followed him to Iowa State. He worked at the cafeteria for his meals also. After one year Gary transferred to Kirkwood College in Cedar Rapids. Once there Gary got a job in an oil station and worked nights and weekends. He didn't get home very much.

Somehow they all managed to get 4 years of college with very little money. I always felt bad that I couldn't help my children more. The family money was not mine to give however. I worked part time and helped when I could with clothes, etc. They did very well with the good educations that they got. Al's Social Security money was what gave them the ability and the incentive to go.

One summer, Gary took a job making T-shirts for a concession stand that followed the county fairs. I didn't want to see him go. I was sure that something would happen to him or his money. He pulled a trailer behind his old car to put his materials in. It was the same company where Creighton had worked for a while at college. He said that the hardest part was living in the dirt. He slept in or next to his car every night. He called one night and said that he'd had enough and was coming home. The next day I expected to see him but he was working the weekend in Ames. I called his boss in Ames. Gary was very put out with me but I was very glad to see him come home. I didn't think anything good could come of it. He said that the carnival people all protected each other and their money.

That was the summer that Creighton hitchhiked to North Carolina to spend the summer at Dan's. He got a job at a McDonald's there. My brothers all hitchhiked and all the servicemen hitchhiked during the war so I didn't think much of it. I had seen a lot of it during the depression and the war. But Creighton ran into some difficult situations that could have turned out badly. He never told me all of the things that happened on that trip.

Dan helped Colleen get a job in Montgomery Ward in Cedar Rapids and that was the start of her living there.

They all left home at 17. It was hard to see them go, and go so young. But there was nothing to hold them in Elma. I felt a great loss as they left home. The house was empty of children.

I was asked to take part in a foster grandmother program with the public school. I had a friend who taught 4th grade, with 32 students. I stayed with that class for 3 years. I did bulletin boards, corrected papers and other clerical work. I enjoyed it very much and I got

MARY CARROLL

$2.00/hr with lunch and transportation. It was a paid-volunteer program. It was something to do and not retire all at once. We worked 4 hours a day. I quit when I was 62. Joe had left the Equity two years earlier when he reached 62.

JOE

Joe had come into a family of five. It was quite a change for him. Now there were just the two of us. Dad was gone and all of the kids were busy and away with their lives. It was quite a transition for me too. We had never really had time alone. So we started to do some travelling. Until we were physically unable to go, we got quite a bit of travelling done. My brothers Gene and Ray had moved out to Arizona and we were able to visit them several times. The first time Gene was well enough to show us all around Phoenix. We drove once with the Fangmans too and also went to Arizona for Gene's funeral in 1981. When Ray died his body was brought back to Wisconsin and buried with family that he had there.

We went to the Black Hills in South Dakota and down to Fort Collins with the Fangmans. Some weekends we went to Lake City, Mn and fished with the Fangmans and the Strattans. When the Fangmans went to a retirement community in Arkansas, we went there too.

About this time some of the banks were offering trips to their senior groups who were bank patrons. We took quite a few tours, going to Washington DC, Nashville, Canada, Mackinac Island and California. Joe and I went with Dan to California for Becky's college graduation from Marymount College in Southern California.

I always said to Joe that if we live to be married 25 years then we would celebrate. We planned to go back to the Ozarks with a bank trip which fell on our anniversary. Sadly Joe passed away 3 months before the trip.

Joe was not feeling well after he got to be 70. His back bothered him a lot and he lost interest in a lot of things. He spent some part of every day at Mort's gas station talking to the other retirees. These fellows all had laments, complaints and regrets so they didn't make very good company. Joe spent a lot of time on the davenport because his back felt better that way.

We had lived all this time in the building that I had made into a rest home. We had several real estate people trying to sell it for us with no luck. We thought we would move to Osage if we could sell. The neighbors next door always indicated that they wanted the place. It was a hard property to sell because it was a home and not a business. Also they did not want to buy from the realtors because they wanted it for less. But Dan had been doing a wonderful job selling in business so I asked him to try to sell it to the neighbors. One 4th of July he and Joyce were in Elma and he sold it in one day. Joe had never really thought it would be sold and did not really have any plans to leave. He had lived in Elma all of his life and didn't really want to move.

I decided that Osage wasn't the direction to go, as it was 20 miles west of Elma. Gary and his family had moved 45 miles to the east, to Decorah. I felt we should go in that direction but Decorah didn't feel right to me. We drove around one Sunday but I didn't like to think about driving in the hills if it was icy. When we moved to Cresco we figured it would be close to Decorah too.

In a short time I found a house that was just what I wanted. We put some money on it. They accepted our bid and we had bought it before we had a chance to even look at anything else. I knew it was the house I wanted to retire in. The buyers didn't want anyone to know about the sale until the deal was signed. Our friends were very surprised when we had a place and were going to move.

I don't think Joe ever really wanted to leave Elma. He didn't say much but he had a brother and a sister there, though we never saw them much. But I was going home and I was happy about it.

I had no such regrets about leaving Elma. I hadn't wanted to go there in the first place. We couldn't buy anything there anymore. We didn't drive that readily. There was no longer a doctor there. I had had to keep a list of things we needed and could only go to other towns when the weather was good. Also a lot of my friends had gone too, leaving to stay with their families. So I was pleased when we got to Cresco because I had a lot of friends there already. We went on a few bus trips while we were there. Joe met some people he used to know and started going to Sunday dinners and playing cards again. He really enjoyed it in Cresco. He liked the church and he took interest in things again.

However both Joe and I had medical problems in Cresco. During a check up a spot was found on one of my lungs, though it turned out to be a fungus, not cancer. I had surgery and it took a long time to regain my strength but I was lucky. Joe had polyps removed from his colon, though these were not cancer either. He was very sick with them and during the medical evaluations the doctors found heart issues too.

In 1992 the last time that Joe went to the doctor, the doctor gave him nitroglycerin for his heart. He didn't look too good but said he felt better. Not long after I awoke to a ringing telephone. I got up and answered the call but when I went back to bed I found that Joe was dead. He had the kind of heart trouble that closed off the veins by hardening them. It was not the kind where they could have operated and cleaned the veins. He had told me he had a stomach ache when he went to bed. I remember that at 4am he was awake. I asked him if he felt any better but he said his stomach was still bothering him. He turned over and said, "I love you." Those were the last words he ever said.

MARY CARROLL

WIDOWED

Being a widow when you are young leaves you feeling that your dreams and plans are all gone forever. Being a widow when you are middle-aged makes you feel that you have been left alone with a family to care for. Being a widow when you are old is a different thing. This time you really are alone. You have to start over. You are responsible for the bills, the home and the car. You are alone at night. You are alone when you are sick. You are no longer one of the couples.

Joe left me with enough money to take care of me for the rest of my time. I have no financial problems and I am very fortunate.

Something else has happened late in my life that makes it easier and more worth living. I have found a friend who is now a companion and a dear friend. It is too late now for new commitments but it is wonderful to know that someone is near and someone cares. He likes to drive and we have Sunday drives to find a nice place to eat. Sometimes we just go to get ice cream in the evening.

I have had a god life. I have had many people who loved me. I have a wonderful family who are as close as the phone. I have a lovely house that is small enough for me to take care of. I have very good friends. My money is there for me to use as I wish. I'll ask for no more.

This is the end of my story!

MARY CARROLL

Endnotes

[i] ***Robert Emmet*** (4 March 1778 – 20 September 1803) was an Irish nationalist and Republican, orator and rebel leader. He led an abortive rebellion against British rule in 1803 and was captured, tried and executed for high treason.

[ii] Milwaukee Road train from Davenport to St. Paul.

[iii] ***Protivin, IA***: The first Czech settlers arrived around 1855 and established themselves because the landscape reminded them of their home region. The community was and is predominately Catholic and they built their own church in 1878 which was the town's first structure.[2] Protivin holds an annual weekend festival known as Czech Days each August where the town's Czech heritage is celebrated. The event draws people from throughout Howard and Chickasaw Counties.

[iv] ***Our Lady of the Assumption Catholic Church & School***, founded 1858, 229 Third Ave W
116 Third St E., Cresco, IA 52136. This church merged with St Joseph`s to form Notre Dame Parish.

[v] The ***Overland Automobile*** "runabout" was founded by Claude Cox in 1903 in Terre Haute, IN. In 1905, he relocated the Overland Automobile Company to Indianapolis, Indiana. In 1908, Overland Motors was purchased by John North Willys. In 1912, it was renamed Willys-Overland. Overlands continued to be produced until 1926 when the marque was succeeded by the Willys Whippet. More recently the Overland name was acquired by American Motors, later Chrysler. Jeep has recently re-introduced the Overland name on a line of Jeep automobiles (2012)

[vi] ***Roosevelt*** was a brand of American automobile that was manufactured by the Marmon Motor Car Company of Indianapolis, Indiana, USA, during model years 1929 and 1930. The Roosevelt was named after President Theodore Roosevelt and designed to be priced as an "affordable" automobile.

[vii] Around 1915, ***Funk Bros***. of Illinois developed a hybrid corn, Funk's Tribred. In the late 1930s the company also developed another hybrid variety, the Funk's G-Series Hybrid, named after brother Gene Funk.

Funk's G-Hybrid and the Funk Brothers Seed Company in their day were the world's leading producers of hybrid corn. In 1967 Funk Bros. Seed Co. was purchased by CPC International, Inc. The company has since merged with several others: AstraZeneca and Syngenta which is still producing agricultural products.

viii The **Farm Credit Act of 1933** established the Farm Credit System (FCS) as a group of cooperative lending institutions to provide short-, intermediate-, and long-term loans for agricultural purposes.

ix In 1933, President Franklin D. Roosevelt appointed *Henry A. Wallace* United States Secretary of Agriculture in his Cabinet, a post his father, Henry Cantwell Wallace, had occupied from 1921 to 1924. Wallace had been a liberal Republican, but he supported Roosevelt's New Deal and soon switched to the Democratic Party. Wallace served as Secretary of Agriculture until September 1940, when he resigned, having been nominated for Vice President as Roosevelt's running mate in the 1940 presidential election. During his tenure as U.S. Secretary of Agriculture he ordered a very unpopular strategy of slaughtering pigs and plowing up cotton fields in rural America to drive the price of these commodities back up in order to improve American farmers' financial situation. He also advocated the ever-normal granary concept.

x *Franklin Delano Roosevelt,* also known by his initials, **FDR**, was the 32nd President of the United States (1933–1945) leading the United States during a time of worldwide economic crisis and world war. FDR defeated incumbent Republican Herbert Hoover in November 1932, at the depth of the Great Depression. FDR's persistent optimism and activism contributed to a renewal of the national spirit, reflecting his victory over paralytic illness to become the longest serving president in U.S. history.

xi The **Rural Electrification Administration (REA)**, one of the New Deal agencies created under President Franklin Delano Roosevelt. The REA was created on May 11, 1935, with the primary goal of promoting rural electrification.[j] In the 1930s, the U.S. lagged significantly behind Europe in providing electricity to rural areas due to the unwillingness of power companies to serve farmsteads. In 1934, less than 11% of US farms had electricity. (In Germany and France that same year, nearly 90% of farms had electricity.) By 1942, nearly 50% of US farms had electricity, and by 1952 almost all US farms had electricity.

xii **Prohibition in the United States** was a national ban on the sale, manufacture, and transportation of alcohol, in place from 1919 to 1933.

xiii Low-point beer, which is often known in America as **"three-two beer"** or "3 point 2 brew", is beer that contains 3.2% alcohol by weight (equivalent to 4% ABV).

xiv Niagara Cave is one of the largest caves in the Midwest and features ancient fossils older than some dinosaurs, a 60-foot waterfall in the largest room in the cave, and a wedding chapel. There have been over 400 weddings in the cave since it opened. Outside the cave there are 10 acres of picnic grounds, a sluice box where tourists can mine for gems and fossils.

xv The **Civilian Conservation Corps** (**CCC**) was a public work relief program that operated from 1933 to 1942 in the United States for unemployed, unmarried men from relief families, ages 17–23. A part of the New Deal of President Franklin D. Roosevelt, it provided unskilled manual labor jobs related to the conservation and development of natural resources in rural lands owned by federal, state and local governments. The CCC was designed to provide employment for young men in relief families who had difficulty finding jobs during the Great Depression while at the same time implementing a general natural resource conservation program in every state and territory. Maximum enrollment at any one time was 300,000; in nine years 2.5 million young men participated.

The American public made the CCC the most popular of all the New Deal programs.[1] Principal benefits of an individual's enrollment in the CCC included improved physical condition, heightened morale, and increased employability. Of their pay of $30 a month, $25 went to their parents.

During the time of the CCC, volunteers planted nearly 3 billion trees to help reforest America, constructed more than 800 parks nationwide and upgraded most state parks, updated forest fire fighting methods, and built a network of service buildings and public roadways in remote areas.

xvi A **normal school** is a school created to train high school graduates to be teachers. Its purpose is to establish teaching standards or *norms*, hence its name. Most such schools are now called **teachers' colleges**; however, in some places, the term *normal school* is still used.

xvii The Armstice Day Blizzard: The morning of 11 November 1940 brought with it unseasonably high temperatures. By early afternoon temperatures had warmed in lower to middle 60s °F over most of the affected region. However, as the day wore on conditions quickly deteriorated. Temperatures dropped sharply, winds picked up, and rain, followed by sleet, and then snow began to fall.

The result was a raging blizzard that would last into the next day. **Snowfalls of up to 27 inches**, winds of 50 to 80 mph, 20-foot snow drifts, and 50-degree Fahrenheit temperature drops were common over parts of the states of Nebraska, South Dakota, Iowa, Minnesota, Wisconsin, and Michigan. **In Minnesota, 27 inches** of snow fell at Collegeville, and the Twin Cities **recorded 16 inches**. Transportation and communications were crippled, which exacerbated finding the dead and injured. The **Armistice Day Blizzard** ranks #2 in Minnesota's list of top-5 weather events of the 20th century.

xviii Bergfalk Furniture of Cresco, IA. Later acquired by DA Larson Furniture.

xix Polashek's Locker Service Inc. of Protivin, Iowa, was founded in 1983 by Paul and Judy Polashek. This is the successor to the noted meat processor.

xx **The Victor Talking Machine Company** (1901–1929) was an American corporation, the leading American producer of phonographs and phonograph records and one of the leading phonograph companies in the world at the time. In September 1906, Johnson and his engineers designed a new line of phonographs with the turntable and amplifying horn tucked away inside a wooden cabinet. This was not done for reasons of audio fidelity, but for visual aesthetics. The intention was to produce a phonograph that looked less like a piece of machinery and more like a piece of furniture. These internal horn machines, trademarked with the name **Victrola**, were first marketed to the public in August of 1906 and were an immediate hit. Victrolas became by far the most popular brand of home phonograph, and sold in great numbers until the end of the 1920s. RCA Victor continued to market phonographs with the "Victrola" name until the early 1970s.

xxi The **rhythm band** is one of the primary methods of introducing children to playing music. Children are given maracas, tambourines, bells, rhythm sticks and other idiophones with which to beat out a simple rhythm while the teacher plays a song, usually on the piano. Rhythm bands are usually found in nursery schools or kindergartens. Melodic instruments are introduced to the children in the first or second year of regular school.

xxii *Spillville Iowa* boasts a strong cultural and musical history. The Czech composer Antonín Dvořák spent the summer of 1893 in Spillville, where he composed two of his most famous chamber works, including the String Quartet in F ("The American"). Spillville is also the site of the Inwood Ballroom, established in 1920 and the destination of several popular 20th century musicians such as Louis Armstrong, Glenn Miller, Guy Lombardo.

xxiii ***Your Hit Parade***, is an American radio and television music program that was broadcast from 1935 to 1955 on radio, and seen from 1950 to 1959 on television. It was sponsored by American Tobacco's Lucky Strike cigarettes. During this 24-year run, the show had 19 orchestra leaders and 52 singers or groups. Many listeners and viewers casually referred to the show as *The Hit Parade*.

xxiv The **Selective Training and Service Act of 1940** instituted national conscription in peacetime, requiring registration of all men between 21 and 45, with selection for one year's service by a national lottery. The term of service was extended by one year in August 1941. After Pearl Harbor the STSA was further amended (December 19, 1941), extending the term of service to the duration of the war and six months and requiring the registration of all men 18 to 64 years of age. In the massive draft of World War II, 50 million men from 18 to 45 were registered, 36 million classified, and 10 million inducted.

xxv The **Ford Model A** of 1928–1931 was the second huge success for the Ford Motor Company. First produced on October 20, 1927, it replaced the venerable Model T, which had been produced for 18 years. This new Model was designated as a 1928 model and was available in four standard colors, but not black. By February 1929, one million Model As had been sold, and by July 1929, two million. In March 1930, Model A sales hit three million, and there were nine body styles available. The Model A was produced through 1931.

xxvi Civilians first received **ration books**—War Ration Book Number One, or the "Sugar Book"—on 4 May 1942, through more than 100,000 schoolteachers, PTA groups, and other volunteers.

xxvii **2-C**: Registrant deferred because of agricultural occupation.

xxviii By 1942, the SSS moved away from administrative selection by its more than 4,000 local boards to a system of lottery selection. Rather than filling quotas by local selection, the boards now ensured proper processing of men selected by the lottery. On 5 December 1942 a presidential executive order changed the age range for the draft from 21-45 to 18-38, and ended voluntary enlistment. Paul V. McNutt, head of the War Manpower Commission, estimated that the changes would increase the ratio of men drafted from one out of nine to one out of five.

xxix **4-F**: Registrant not acceptable for military service. To be eligible for Class 4-F, a registrant must have been found not qualified for service in the Armed Forces by a Military Entrance Processing Station (MEPS) under the established physical, mental, or moral standards.

xxx **KP duty** is "**kitchen police**" or "**kitchen patrol**" work under the kitchen staff assigned to junior U.S. enlisted military personnel.

xxxi According to Closing the Literacy Gap in American Business: A Guide for Trainers and Human Resource Specialists , in WWI, 25% of draftees were found to be illiterate. The military rejected nearly 750,000 potential draftees due to "educational deficiencies."

xxxii In December 1944, the Imperial Japanese Navy organized the 1st Submarine Flotilla and 631st *Kokutai* (Air Corps), with Captain Tatsunoke Ariizumi commanding both units. The force consisted of *I-400*, *I-401* and two AM-class subs, *I-13* and *I-14*, which were smaller and carried two Seiran bomber aircraft each, for a total of 10 Seiran bombers. In other words, *I-401* wasn't just a major offensive weapon in a submarine fleet used to playing defense—it was actually the world's first purpose-built underwater aircraft carrier.

In March 1945, Vice Adm. Jisaburo Ozawa, vice chief of the navy general staff, toyed with a plan to use the Seirans to unleash biological weapons on a U.S. West Coast city in revenge for the firebombing of Tokyo. The notorious Japanese Unit 731 had already conducted successful experiments in Manchuria using rats infected with bubonic plague and other diseases to kill Chinese citizens. But the operation was canceled later that month by General Yoshijiro Umezu, chief of the army general staff, who declared, "Germ warfare against the United States would escalate to war against all humanity." **Instead, the Japanese decided to target the** *Panama Canal.*

On August 28, 1945, the USS *Segundo*, a *Balao*-class submarine with commanding officer, Lieutenant Commander S.L. Johnson intercepted the submarine fleet on their way to attack the ***Panama Canal***,13 days *after* Japan's surrender announcement.

xxxiii Soldiers at Polk participated in the ***Louisiana Maneuvers***, which were designed to test U.S. troops preparing for World War II. Until 1939, the Army had mostly been an infantry force with supporting artillery, engineer, and cavalry units. Few units had been motorized or mechanized. As U.S. involvement in World War II became more likely, the Army recognized the need to modernize the service. But it also needed large-scale maneuvers to test a fast-growing, inexperienced force. That is where Fort Polk and the Louisiana Maneuvers came in. The Maneuvers involved half a million soldiers in 19 Army Divisions, and took place over 3,400 square miles (8,800 km²) in August and September 1941. The Maneuvers gave Army leadership the chance to test a new doctrine that stressed the need for both mass and mobility.

xxxiv (Possibly) The 84th Infantry Division (known as The Rail Splitters) was activated on 15 October 1942. It embarked on 20 September 1944 and arrived in the United Kingdom on 1 October, for additional training. The division landed on Omaha Beach, 1–4 November 1944, and moved to the vicinity of Gulpen, the Netherlands, 5–12 November. The division entered combat, 18 November, with an attack on Geilenkirchen, Germany, as part of the larger offensive in the Roer Valley, north of Aachen.

xxxv Alexandria and Central Louisiana were the center of the maooivo Louisiana Maneuvers staged just prior to World War II. A major focal point in the maneuvers was Camp Claiborne.

xxxvi The **Studebaker Cham**pion is an automobile which was produced by the Studebaker Corporation of South Bend, Indiana from 1939 model until 1958. For its size, it was one of the lightest cars of its era The Champion was one of Studebaker's best-selling models by virtue of its low price (US$660 for the two-door business coupe in 1939), durable engine and styling. During World War II, Champions were coveted for their high mileage at a time when gas was rationed in the United States. The Champion was phased out in 1958 in preparation for the introduction of the 1959 Studebaker Lark.

xxxvii **Cuba Libre:** This drink was once viewed as exotic, with its dark syrup, made from cola nuts and coca. As Charles H. Baker, Jr. points out in his *Gentlemen's Companion* of 1934, the Cuba Libre "caught on everywhere throughout the American South ... filtered through the North and West," aided by the ample supply of its ingredients. The drink gained further popularity in the United States after the Andrews Sisters recorded a song (in 1945) named after the drink's ingredients, "Rum and Coca-Cola". Cola and rum were both cheap at the time and this also contributed to the widespread popularity of the concoction.[5]

xxxviii In the four years of civil war **1861-65** the South was the primary battleground, with all but two of the major battles taking place on Southern soil. Union forces relentlessly squeezed the Confederacy, capturing the border states in 1861, the Tennessee River, the Cumberland River and New Orleans in 1862, and the Mississippi River in 1863. The Southern transportation system depended primarily on river and coastal traffic by boat; both were shut down by the Union Navy. The small railroad system virtually collapsed, so that by 1864 internal travel was so difficult that the Confederate economy was crippled.

The South suffered much more than the North overall, as the Union strategy of attrition warfare meant that Lee could not replace his casualties, and the total war waged by Sherman, Sheridan and other Union armies devastated the infrastructure and caused widespread poverty and distress. The Confederacy suffered military losses of 95,000 men killed in action and 165,000 who died of disease, for a total of 260,000, out of a total white Southern population at the time of around 5.5 million. Based on 1860 census figures, 8% of all white males aged 13 to 43 died in the war, including 6% in the North and about 18% in the South. Northern military casualties exceeded Southern casualties in absolute numbers, but were two-thirds smaller in terms of proportion of the population affected.

xxxix **St-Lô**, capital of the department of Manche, France, can be used as one symbol for First U. S. Army's victory in a most difficult and bloody phase of the Campaign of Normandy: the "Battle of the Hedgerows," during the first three weeks of July 1944. St-Lô will be remembered by First Army soldiers as a stubborn struggle for gains too often measured in terms of a few hundred yards, or of two or three fields, conquered against a bitterly resisting enemy. *(CMH Pub 100-13,* Center of Military History, United States Army, Washington, D.C.)

xl Adoption agency or orphanage.

xli By the early 1920's just about every drugstore had a ***soda fountain***. The reason for the explosion of soda fountains was most likely that Prohibition began in 1919 and the soda fountain filled the social void caused by the closing of bars. Many of the fountain drinks made by the early druggists contained cocaine and caffeine. The combination of cocaine and caffeine was used to effectively cure headaches. The problem was that rebound headaches would ensue and the patient would be back frequently for another drink to get rid of the pain. Many druggists even made and marketed their own secret formulations. Many pharmacies began to distance themselves from the bad reputation that developed as result of the "habit forming" products sold from the 1860's through the early 1900's. Jacob Baur, founder of the Liquid Carbonic Company, used the following in an advertisement for one of his soft drinks, "it isn't medicinal, won't cure anything… isn't intoxicating or habit forming – it's just flavory, fruity, snappy, sparkling, delicious." The soda fountain eventually lost the old reputation and became known for serving "soft drinks".

xlii Knights of Columbus Hall, Elma, IA

xliii **Rheumatic fever** is an inflammatory disease that may develop after an infection with *Streptococcus* bacteria (such as strep throat or scarlet fever). The disease can affect the heart, joints, skin, and brain. Rheumatic fever is common worldwide and is responsible for many cases of damaged heart valves.

xliv Florey and Chain succeeded in purifying the ***first penicillin,*** penicillin G procaine in 1942, but it did not become widely available outside Allied military before 1945.

xlv **Brucellosis**, also called **Malta fever**, **Maltese fever**, is a highly contagious zoonosis caused by ingestion of unsterilized milk or meat from infected animals or close contact with their secretions.

xlvi Bergfalk Furniture of Cresco, IA. Later acquired by DA Larson Furniture in 1952.

xlvii The **Meskwaki** are a Native American people often known to outsiders as the **Fox** tribe. They have often been closely linked to the Sauk people. In their own language, the Meskwaki call themselves *Meshkwahkihaki*, which means "the Red-Earths." The tribe coalesced in the St. Lawrence River Valley in Ontario; it later moved to Michigan, Wisconsin, Illinois, and Iowa. In the 19th century, Euro-American colonization and settlement proceeded, forcing resettlement of the people south into the tall grass prairie in the American Midwest. The Meskwaki, within the designation 'Sac and Fox,' currently have reservations in Iowa, Oklahoma, Kansas, and Nebraska. By 1910, the Sac and Meskwaki together totaled only about 1,000 people. By the year 2000, their numbers had increased to nearly 4,000.

The modern Meskwaki Settlement in **Tama County** maintains Casino, tribal schools, tribal courts, and tribal police, and a public works department.

xlviii Then St. Bede College, now **Saint Bede Academy** is a private, four-year, Catholic college-preparatory high school located in Peru, Illinois. The campus buildings and monastery are situated on 200 acres of wooded land. The monastery is home to 32 Benedictine monks who have taken a vow of stability, meaning that they remain at Saint Bede Abbey for their lifetimes. The monks take an active role in the affairs and administration of the academy

xlix Surgeons realized the limitations of the early technique using hypothermia for slowing the metabolism – complex heart repairs take more time and the patient needs blood flow to the body, particularly to the brain. *Brain impairment from oxygen starvation was common.* The patient needs the function of the heart and lungs provided by an artificial means. Doctors at Jefferson Medical School in Philadelphia reported in 1953 the first successful use of external circulation by means of an oxygenator, but he abandoned the method, disappointed by subsequent failures. In 1954 Dr. Lillehei realized a successful series of operations with the controlled cross-circulation technique in which the **patient's mother or father was used** as a 'heart-lung machine'. At the Mayo Clinic in Rochester,

Minnesota surgeons started using a Gibbon type pump-oxygenator in a series of successful operations, and was soon followed by surgeons in various parts of the world.

www.ingramcontent.com/pod-product-compliance
Lightning Source LLC
Chambersburg PA
CBHW031329040426

42443CB00005B/268